Managing
Corporate
Pension Plans

Managing Corporate Pension Plans

The Impacts of Inflation

Dennis E. Logue
Richard J. Rogalski

American Enterprise Institute for Public Policy Research
Washington and London

Dennis E. Logue is professor of business administration and Richard J. Rogalski is finance professor at the Amos Tuck School of Business Administration, Dartmouth College.

Our sincere thanks go to Colin Campbell, Dallas Salisbury, and Arthur Williams III, who read the entire manuscript and offered numerous helpful suggestions. Thanks also go to Russell Greenberg, who helped with the statistical work. Finally, Barbara Haskell and Suzanne Sweet typed the manuscript—many times. To them we express our deep gratitude.

D.E.L. / R.J.R.

Library of Congress Cataloging in Publication Data

Logue, Dennis E.
  Managing corporate pension plans.

  (AEI studies ; 355)
  1. Pension trusts—United States—Investments—Effect of inflation on. I. Rogalski, Richard J. II. Title. III. Series.
HD7105.45.U6L63 1984   332.6'7254   83-25786
ISBN 0-8447-3486-1
ISBN 978-0-8447-3486-6
AEI Studies 355

1 3 5 7 9 10 8 6 4 2

Contents

Foreword

It is widely known that during inflationary periods unforeseen changes in the price level can affect the real returns on financial assets. Since 1965, holders of fixed-dollar assets have incurred substantial losses in real capital because of inflation. The corporate pension system in the United States, mostly composed of fixed-dollar assets, has not been impervious to such losses.

With variable inflation, managers of pension funds must incur the additional costs of improving planning, hedging against possible loss, and replenishing funding requirements. Beneficiaries of the plans lose to inflation through the reduced pension benefits they receive if these benefits are either fixed in nominal terms or dependent on the rate of return obtained by the fund. And the nation as a whole suffers as inflation reduces the net aggregate pension savings available for capital formation, thereby eroding the nation's future real economic output growth.

Dennis E. Logue and Richard J. Rogalski explain the issues and problems created for the corporate pension system. They present empirical evidence to show that during the recent inflationary period market rates of return failed to compensate investors adequately for their loss of purchasing power. As a result the national savings base was reduced and the pension system weakened.

The authors conduct a microanalysis of the investment performance and portfolio strategies of a number of small pension funds to see whether these funds fared any better than the aggregate market. Individual pension funds failed in most cases to keep pace with inflation, but did no worse than other managed portfolios. More important, however, Logue and Rogalski find that actively managed funds—those that attempted to beat inflation by constantly switching among assets—did not do as well as those funds that retained, for the most part, their original portfolios.

To give the reader a better idea of the actual policies and strategies employed by a typical pension fund during an inflationary era, the authors make a case study of a major corporate pension fund. They offer useful suggestions to secure the U.S. corporate pension system against inflation. The most promising of these is the construction of optimal strategies that include futures market contracts in addition to fixed-income and equities to reduce overall real portfolio risks.

This study—one of a number of AEI studies in social security and retirement policies—covers a topic that is obviously important to the social welfare system of this nation. It analyzes private pension investments in terms of their implications for capital formation and real returns to retirees. It also analyzes the contribution that futures markets can make to improve real returns in an inflationary environment. The AEI project to study the economics and regulation of futures markets is a related effort to foster healthy public policy discourse on the role of these market institutions.

WILLIAM J. BAROODY
President
American Enterprise Institute

1
Introduction

The inflation experienced in the United States since the late 1960s has surely had significant effects on the economic status of the country and its citizens. Inflation is typically accompanied by welfare costs that reduce a nation's real economic output and capacity.[1] Inflation also redistributes income and wealth among the members of society, often without regard to their prudence or foresight. In brief, inflation creates substantial problems that must be dealt with during its rampage and often after it subsides.

The corporate pension system in the United States is a victim of inflation. The corporations that sponsor pension plans are victims, since planning for funding has been made increasingly difficult and real (as opposed to nominal) funding requirements have risen. Pension recipients whose real pension benefits (fixed nominal benefits) have been, and continue to be, eroded by inflation are victims too. Current employees covered by pension plans may also be victims, depending on whether other asset holdings have benefited or lost as a consequence. Furthermore, the nation as a whole suffers in that aggregate pension saving is reduced by inflation, and this reduction in funds available for capital formation is not generally offset through increases in other forms of saving.[2]

This study considers the effect of inflation on the corporate pension system. It shows in chapter 2 how the pension system's viability, indeed its desirability and attractiveness to employers and employees, may be reduced through inflation. We show that the failure of capital market rates of return to compensate investors adequately for the erosion of purchasing power is crucial in weakening the corporate pension system. In brief, the relationship between rates of return and inflation more than anything else affects the viability of the pension system.

Chapter 3 summarizes some general evidence regarding the behavior of U.S. investment market returns during periods of inflation. For the last thirty years or so, the evidence shows, nominal rates of return have not fully compensated for losses of purchasing power plus the risk of the investments themselves. During the late 1970s nominal returns failed to compensate for inflation alone. Aggregate market results reveal that financial assets were generally not good inflation hedges. We cannot automatically assume, however, that managed pension fund portfolios did not generate investment returns that kept pace with inflation. The investment performance and portfolio strategies of a small group of pension funds receive detailed attention in chapter 4. The evidence depicts a dismal record. Not only did the typical managed pension fund fail to keep pace with inflation, but many funds were made worse off as a consequence of active management policies. Note, however, that pension funds very likely did no worse than other managed portfolios.

Chapter 5 is a case study of a major corporate pension plan. It describes the attempts made by the sponsoring corporation, an anonymous Fortune 500 firm, to cope with the problem of inflation. The decisions made by this firm are probably no worse and perhaps somewhat better than those of the average firm that produced the kind of results described in the preceding chapter. The case study is informative because it provides some insight into alternative portfolio policies for those who are responsible for making portfolio decisions.

Chapter 6 suggests some policies and objectives by which firms may mitigate the influence of inflation on their pension plans. Although we tender no magical formulas or foolproof advice, we offer as our principal conclusion that reducing trading costs through the use of passive strategies and the construction of optimal portfolios that are tilted toward particular sorts of securities, especially bonds and commodity futures, may lessen the erosion of the purchasing power of pension funds.

Notes

1. Martin Feldstein, "The Welfare Cost of Permanent Inflation and Optimal Short-Run Economic Policy," *Journal of Political Economy*, vol. 87 (August 1979), pp. 749–68.

2. See John A. Turner, "Private Pension Saving and Inflation," manuscript (Washington, D.C.: Social Security Administration, Office of Research and Statistics, 1979).

2
How Inflation Affects Pensions

The effect of inflation on pensions varies with the type of pension plan. Accordingly, this chapter opens with a brief outline of the various types of plans and progresses through an analysis of the effects of inflation on such plans.

Plan Types

There are two principal types of corporate pension plans in use in the United States.[1] The first is the "defined-contribution plan." In this type, the employer contributes a fixed dollar amount or, more generally, a specified fraction of an employee's salary to the plan. The employer makes no guarantees regarding the benefits that an employee will receive. Rather, the employee's pension benefit will be a direct function of the investment performance of the sums invested on the employee's behalf.

The second type of plan is a "defined-benefit plan." For sponsoring corporations, it is far and away the more popular of the two. In such plans the employer promises a specified annual retirement benefit. In the most typical form, this is some percentage of salary multiplied by the number of years of service. If the investment performance of the funds set aside on the employee's behalf exceeds expectations, the employer's future contributions to the pension fund may be reduced. Similarly, if pension fund assets earmarked for a specific employee are inadequate to purchase the annuity that will generate the promised benefits, the employer must make up the deficiency. Hence shareholders directly benefit or suffer from the investment performance of the pension fund.

The principal distinction between these two types of plans is in who bears the risk related to the performance of the pension fund investment portfolio. In defined-contribution plans, employees bear the burden of subnormal investment returns or reap the rewards of supranormal investment returns. In defined-benefit plans, the firm and hence its shareholders are made better or worse off by the invest-

3

ment returns. Another important difference between the two types of plans is the degree of regulation. The Employee Retirement Income Security Act (ERISA) requires defined-benefit plans to bear substantially greater regulatory burdens than defined-contribution plans.

Defined-benefit plans may be further subdivided into two categories, according to the salary basis used in computing benefits. The first is the career-average plan; the second is the final-years plan. In the former, the average salary an employee receives during his career with the firm is multiplied by some percentage and by the number of years with the firm to arrive at the employee's annual retirement benefit. The final-years plan takes as the salary basis the average salary for the final three or five years of an employee's tenure with the corporation. To determine the annual benefit, this amount is multiplied by some percentage and by the number of years of employment.

Inflation's Effects

In a defined-contribution plan, the employee/retiree bears the risk of poor investment performance and inflation. The standard sort of defined-contribution plan has the employer setting aside a specified fraction of the employee's annual salary. Upon retirement this accumulated amount is used to purchase an annuity or a variable annuity, one whose payout depends on the performance of the funds invested.

If an employee's salary keeps pace with inflation and investment returns on the periodically invested sums are sufficient to provide the expected real return as well as to compensate for the erosion of purchasing power due to inflation, the employee's initial retirement benefit will be, in real terms, the amount that was originally anticipated. Upon retirement, if the implied investment return in the annuity contract compensates for inflation or if the actual investment return on a variable annuity is sufficiently high to cover erosion of nominally fixed values, the retiree will be able to realize a constant real annual benefit. If both preretirement and postretirement investment returns are adequate in the sense of providing positive real and full inflationary returns, the effect is a fully indexed pension system.[2] If investment returns are inadequate on either side of the retirement date, of course, real pension benefits are diminished.

At the present time, most organizations with pension plans do not have defined-contribution plans. There are, however, some large and notable exceptions. Many university professors in the United States, for instance, belong to the Teachers Insurance and Annuity Association and the College Retirement Equities Fund (TIAA-CREF). So do many employees of not-for-profit organizations. If preretire-

4

ment investment returns are insufficient (or, for that matter, if salary growth in the particular organization fails to keep pace with inflation), organizations offering defined-contribution plans will come under pressure either to provide supplementary retirement funds or to postpone the mandatory retirement age. The former may, given the now well known financial problems of colleges and universities, be financially impossible. The latter allows for continued salary income, continued buildup of the retirement fund of a member, and a shortened period over which the retirement fund must provide benefits (owing to a lower number of expected years of life after retirement at a later than "normal" age). Unfortunately, this provision may not be desirable from the viewpoint of institutions that are not expanding and that benefit from the innovation and originality that new employees bring.

In defined-contribution plans, even though employers are legally free of risk bearing from subnormal investment fund performance and are not required to alter their contribution rate in response to subnormal performance, there may still be demands on them to make ex post adjustments in benefits if preretirement investment returns fail to keep pace with inflation. If the institutional arrangements accompanying a defined-contribution plan do not put the organization and individual in close contact with each other, however, pressures for ex post adjustment of pension benefits may be weakened.

Most large organizations, particularly business corporations, have defined-benefit plans, which obligate the employer to pay a specified periodic amount to an employee upon retirement. Since these constitute the bulk of private pension plans and are most seriously affected by inflation, the remainder of this book deals with such plans.

As noted above, there are two principal types of defined-benefit plans: (1) those that pay benefits based on career-average salaries and (2) those that pay benefits based on average salaries during the final year or years of an employee's career. In the absence of inflation, the two plans have typically resulted in quite comparable ratios of pension benefits to final salary. Even in the absence of inflation, the average salary of an employee during his career would usually be lower than the average salary during his final years owing to merit raises, promotion, and seniority. Firms offering career-average benefits, however, typically multiply the salary basis by a higher percentage to arrive at the pension benefit than that used by firms that offer final-pay salary bases. As a result, the final pension benefit is about the same in either case. Inflation, unfortunately, changes the picture.

In the absence of inflation, a career-average plan that gives the same weight to earnings thirty years ago and earnings today, for example, is adequate because real, not nominal, figures are being averaged. With inflation, however, legitimate interyear salary comparisons cannot possibly precede significant adjustments for inflation in the salary data. Without those adjustments the real pension benefit received by an employee will be considerably less than anticipated and considerably less than benefits available under a final-salary plan if a worker's salary rose along with the inflation rate. For a variety of reasons having to do with employees' motivation and incentive, some corporations strive to keep future pension benefits even with inflation. (The firm described in chapter 5 is one of these, even though it uses a career-average plan.)

There are several ways in which the real benefits of a career-average plan can be kept comparable to those of a final-years plan, which nearly automatically, by virtue of the relation between a worker's salary in the final years and inflation, adjusts for inflation during the employee's career. The first is periodic adjustment of the percentage that is multiplied by the career-average salary to calculate benefits. The firm might increase the percentage used in the pension benefit formula from 2 percent to 2.25 percent, for example. The second is ex post indexation of historical salaries. Here the employer would inflate prior years' salaries to put them on the same nominal basis as current salaries. The standard pension formula can then be applied. The third and seemingly most common way of coping with the problem is abandonment of the career-average approach in favor of a final-pay approach.[3] This resolves the problem of providing the promised amount of real retirement benefits in relation to final pay.

Table 1 shows, for a large sample of firms, the substantial shift that has occurred from career-average to final-average compensation. Table 2 shows a significant trend toward the use of shorter periods for calculating final-average compensation. Such shifts help protect employees from a decline in the real value of their expected pension benefits at the time of their retirement. Shifts will not, however, protect them from inflation during the retirement period, since the nominal retirement benefit is fixed and will be unaffected by the investment performance of the pension fund. Moreover, they will not fully protect the employee from inflation during the years in the salary basis period, but final-average plans certainly do better than career-average plans in this regard. Note finally that although the shift from career-average to final-average compensation favors employees in the event of inflation, corporate pension contributions must necessarily be higher in nominal terms than they would otherwise be to fund the higher benefits.

In contrast to these trends, some plans, for example, the American Telephone and Telegraph plan, have gone the other way—from

TABLE 1

DISTRIBUTION OF DEFINED-BENEFIT PENSION PLANS, BY COMPENSATION
BASIS, 1950–1975
(percent)

Compensation Basis	1970–75	1965–70	1960–65	1956–59	1953–55	1950–52
All benefits based on career-average compensation	22	35	45	56	62	72
All benefits based on final-average compensation	54	39	31	27	26	18
Regular benefits based on career-average compensation, minimum benefits based on final-average compensation	16	20	16	12	6	4
Benefits based in part on career-average compensation and in part on final-average compensation	8	6	5	2	1	—
Other	0	0	3	3	5	6
Total	100	100	100	100	100	100

SOURCES: Bankers Trust Company, *1975 Study of Corporate Pension Plans; 1965 Study of Industrial Retirement Plans; A Study of Industrial Retirement Plans* (1956 ed.). Adapted from Alicia H. Munnell, "The Impact of Inflation on Private Pensions" (Paper presented at the Southern Economic Meetings, Washington, D.C., 1978).

final pay to career average. The motive for such a move seems to be greater control over pension plan costs. That may come at the expense of preventing employees' expected pension benefits from keeping as close pace with inflation in the future as they have in the past.

We might ask why firms care whether initial (and sometimes even continuing) pension benefits remain roughly constant in real terms. In

7

TABLE 2

Distribution of Pension Plans, by Length of Final-Average Compensation Base, 1956–1975

(percent)

Years in Final-Average Compensation Base	1970–75	1965–70	1960–65	1956–59
3	2	1	—	—
5	93	77	57	53
10	4	15	37	41
Other	1	7	6	6
Total	100	100	100	100

Sources: Bankers Trust Company, *1975 Study of Corporate Pension Plans; 1965 Study of Industrial Retirement Plans; A Study of Industrial Retirement Plans* (1956 ed.). Adapted from Munnell, "The Impact of Inflation."

inflationary times firms (hence shareholders) could save money by staying with career-average plans or long-period final-pay plans. The answer probably lies in the underlying reasons for offering pension plans.

The most compelling reason for corporate pension plans is the incentive effect coupled with tax-deferral advantages of corporate pension plans.[4] Alternative explanations rely on corporate paternalism—pension payments are gifts—and a deferred-wage theory, which holds that pension payments are usually merely wages paid in retirement. The former notion does not explain very much; indeed, its validity is contradicted by the existence of pension contracts. The latter conception seems also to be unrealistic in that the vesting provisions of most pension plans require employees to work a specified minimum number of years before being eligible for a pension. If the deferred-wage theory were correct, firms would be unable to avoid payment of the deferred wage through the vesting provision. In contrast, vesting provisions and other requirements for qualification suggest that pension benefits are intended as an inducement to remain with a particular company. They serve to encourage an employee to work diligently and avoid dismissal so as to qualify for pensions.

If inflation were to be allowed to erode initial retirement benefits, the work and incentive effects of pension plans as a type of compensation would be eroded. Because of the importance to firms of these incentive effects, corporations are willing to increase their contributions to corporate pension plans to compensate employees for inflation during their careers as well as to make up for inadequate pension fund performance.

With both career-average and final-average compensation plans, the magnitude of required corporate cash contributions will be dictated principally by the promised level of benefits and the investment performance of the funds. Accounting methods and actuarial funding methods may influence the pattern and timing of the contributions, but investment performance remains the major issue once benefit goals have been specified. If investment returns do not keep pace with inflation, the firm must make up the deficiency between the amount necessary to purchase the promised annuity and the amount actually available. The greater the difference between anticipated investment returns (which include a real component plus full compensation for inflation) and the actual return, the greater the additional amount the firm must devote to pension fund contributions. All else equal, investment performance that is below par increases the magnitude of the firm's pension liability and hence reduces the value of the shareholders' investment. As Alicia Munnell has shown, the greater the difference between the inflation rate and the nominal return on the portfolio, the more the contribution rate as a percentage of salary must rise.[5] Although illustrations are stylized and do not accurately describe the way plans work, they present an informative and reasonably accurate portrayal of the consequences of inflation. Munnell has also shown that the contribution rate must rise by more than the single-period difference between inflation and nominal returns because of the compounding effect of the difference.

Table 3 shows the results of Thomas Hoffman's simulations based on formulas that are similar though not identical to Munnell's.[6] The figures in the table show the ratio of the accumulated pension fund to final salary for various contribution rates. (Again, the example is stylized—contribution rates shown far exceed those commonly used in practice, which average roughly 8 percent. The exaggeration, however, merely underscores the impact of inflation.)

For contribution rates of 10, 15, and 20 percent, the ratio of the fund accumulated to final salary is shown for different nominal return/salary inflation differentials and for different numbers of years of contributions. The effect of inadequate returns is dramatic. For example, with a 10 percent contribution rate, the ratio of the accumulated fund to final salary can, for a forty-year contribution period, range from 2.4 to 7.4, depending on the relation between investment returns and the rate of salary inflation. This relation significantly affects the amount by which the fund for a particular employee must be augmented to provide a particular retirement benefit.

TABLE 3

ESTIMATES OF THE RATIO OF THE ACCUMULATED FUND TO FINAL SALARY

Years of Contribution	Rate of Return minus Rate of Salary Increase						
	− 3	− 2	− 1	0	1	2	3
10 percent contribution rate							
15	1.24	1.32	1.40	1.50	1.60	1.72	1.85
20	1.55	1.68	1.83	2.00	2.19	2.41	2.66
25	1.82	2.01	2.24	2.50	2.80	3.17	3.60
30	2.05	2.31	2.62	3.00	3.45	4.01	4.69
35	2.26	2.59	2.99	3.50	4.12	4.93	5.94
40	2.43	2.83	3.34	4.00	4.83	5.94	7.39
15 percent contribution rate							
15	1.86	1.98	2.11	2.25	2.40	2.58	2.77
20	2.33	2.52	2.75	3.00	3.28	3.62	3.99
25	2.73	3.02	3.35	3.75	4.21	4.76	5.41
30	3.08	3.47	3.94	4.50	5.17	6.01	7.04
35	3.39	3.88	4.49	5.25	6.19	7.39	8.92
40	3.65	4.25	5.02	6.00	7.25	8.91	11.09
20 percent contribution rate							
15	2.49	2.64	2.81	3.00	3.21	3.43	3.69
20	3.11	3.37	3.66	4.00	4.38	4.81	5.31
25	3.65	4.03	4.48	5.00	5.62	6.33	7.18
30	4.12	4.64	5.25	6.00	6.91	7.99	9.34
35	4.53	5.19	5.99	7.00	8.26	9.82	11.83
40	4.89	5.69	6.70	8.00	9.68	11.83	14.69

SOURCE: Hoffman, "Retirement Funding."

An additional problem associated with inflation is the postretirement decline in real pension benefits that results from a fixed nominal benefit. Most firms that offer defined-benefit plans are obligated to provide only a fixed nominal retirement benefit. Yet, if there is inflation during the retirement period, the real value of the retirement benefit may be considerably less at the end of the period than at the beginning. This is a possible cause of concern to pension-offering firms because current employees' awareness of the probable erosion in their real pension benefits after retirement seriously weakens the incentive effects associated with corporate plans.

Current employees may extrapolate the experiences of past retirees and adjust their expectations of pension benefits downward. Similarly, since social security benefits and federal government pensions

TABLE 4

INFLATION-ADJUSTED REPLACEMENT RATES, BY AGE AND INCOME LEVEL,
WITH 4 PERCENT INFLATION

Final Year's Pay (dollars)		After-Tax Benefits[a] (dollars)	Inflation-Adjusted Replacement Rate by Age (percent)			
Before tax	After tax		65	70	75	80
7,500	6,640	5,200	78	74	71	68
15,000	11,930	9,500	80	74	69	65
30,000	21,900	15,100	69	61	55	50
50,000	33,440	21,950	66	57	50	44

NOTE: Estimates include social security and pension benefits.
a. At age sixty-five.
SOURCES: *Business Roundtable Study of Retirement Benefit Levels, Costs, and Issues*, prepared by Towers, Perrin, Forster & Crosby, Inc., August 1978; these are estimates for single workers retiring in 1979 at age sixty-five with thirty years of service under a pension plan with a benefit of 1.67 percent times high-five-year average pay times years of service, less 1.67 percent times applicable OASI benefit times years of service; it is assumed that the value of private benefits declines with an inflation rate of 4 percent. This table was taken from Employee Benefit Research Institute, *Retirement Income Policy: Considerations for Effective Decision Making* (Washington, D.C., 1980).

are indexed, one would exhibit a growing demand for private pensions that compensate for inflation.

Table 4 shows the decline in the real value of replacement rates (the ratio of postretirement benefits to final after-tax salary) for various salary levels, assuming a moderate 4 percent inflation rate. The examples in this table include social security benefits that are indexed; so the estimated erosion in real after-tax replacement rates is mitigated to some extent, especially for low-income employees. The replacement rate drops significantly as the retiree ages. At higher inflation rates the decline in the real value of retirement income would be much larger. Over the past few years, with inflation running in the range of 6 to 14 percent, retired workers have suffered substantial declines in their post-tax real benefits.

Firms providing pensions may respond to the effects of inflation on retirement pensions in several ways. First and most obviously, they may completely ignore the situation. As we have mentioned, this approach risks reducing pension fund incentive effects. Second, firms may make ad hoc adjustments in their benefits to reduce the erosive effects of inflation on real pension benefits. Many firms, including the corporation in our case study, have taken such action.

TABLE 5
NUMBER OF YEARS A PENSION FUND WILL LAST
IF BENEFITS RISE WITH INFLATION

Annuity Rate of Return minus Inflation Rate	Ratio of Total Accumulation at Retirement to Initial Benefit						
	8	10	12	14	16	18	20
−3	7.2	8.6	9.9	11.1	12.1	12.9	13.6
−2	7.5	9.1	10.7	12.1	13.5	14.8	16.0
−1	7.7	9.6	11.4	13.1	14.8	16.5	18.1
0	8.0	10.0	12.0	14.0	16.0	18.0	20.0
1	8.2	10.4	12.6	14.8	17.2	19.5	21.9
2	8.5	10.8	13.4	15.0	18.6	21.5	24.6
3	8.7	11.4	14.0	17.0	20.6	23.9	27.4

SOURCE: Hoffman, "Retirement Funding."

These firms arbitrarily raise benefits from time to time, even though they are under no obligation to do so. If the investment performance of the pension fund has not been adequate, however, additional sums must be taken from the corporation's shareholders. A third strategy is full or partial indexation of pension benefits. As long as investment returns exceed the expected real or actuarial return by the inflation rate, such a strategy will not affect corporate contributions to the fund or the corporation's contingent liabilities. As we discuss later, investment returns have simply not been adequate to permit use of this strategy. If investment returns are not adequate, promises of indexed benefits can be costly. A fourth approach is to shift to a defined-contribution plan. The pension received under such a plan would depend directly on investment returns whether or not these returns compensated for inflation.

Table 5 illustrates in another way the dimensions of the problem of the effect of inflation on pensions. It assumes a benefit equal to 35 percent of final salary and a contribution rate of 20 percent of salary and shows the number of years for which a single employee's planned pension accumulation would last if the pension were indexed to provide constant real benefits. The figures are presented for various combinations of differences between the actual nominal rate of return on the pension accumulation and the inflation rate and for ratios of total accumulations at time of retirement to initial benefits.

Table 5 also shows that the smaller the difference between investment returns and inflation, the quicker the accumulation runs out when benefits are fixed in real, not nominal, terms. Note that to achieve initial fund-to-benefit ratios of, say, 12 or more requires a contribution rate of approximately 10 percent for forty years when investment returns equal inflation. For worse returns, higher rates are necessary. To the extent that contribution rates fall below this level or returns are lower than expected, pension fund accumulations provide indexed benefits for only short periods of time—unless, of course, corporations are willing to increase the portion of cash flows allocated to pension funds to provide cost-of-living adjustments.

Conclusion

This chapter has demonstrated that the current issues regarding pensions and inflation are in large measure attributable to the difference between the inflation rate and the rate of return on pension fund investments. If investment returns are sufficiently high, the sponsoring corporation can be generous and maintain real benefits. Workers' pension benefits can easily be protected from inflation through final salary formulas or by ad hoc adjustments in career-average pension benefit formulas; actual corporate contributions can be kept within estimated bounds; and cost-of-living increases can be granted to retired workers so that the real value of pension-benefit incentives can be maintained. If investment returns are inadequate, even if constant real pension benefits work to the advantage of shareholders—through motivation and retention of employees and reduction of labor turnover costs—either the cash flow anticipated by shareholders must be diverted, or pension benefits must be allowed to erode.

It is crucially important to gauge the capital market's response to inflation and to assess the actual investment performance of pension fund portfolios. If satisfactory returns have been achieved, industrial pension policy can be formulated without much regard for inflation. On the other hand, if that is not the case, the pension program of many, perhaps all, companies may require drastic overhaul to take into account the realities of inflation.[7]

Notes

1. For a fuller description of corporate pension plans, see Dennis E. Logue, *Legislative Influence on Corporate Pension Plans* (Washington, D.C.: American Enterprise Institute, 1979).

2. See James E. Pesando and Samuel A. Rea, Jr., *Public and Private Pensions in Canada* (Toronto: University of Toronto Press, 1977), chap. 4, pp. 49–65.

3. See Logue, *Legislative Influence*, p. 44.

4. For an elaboration, see ibid., chap. 3.

5. Alicia H. Munnell, "The Impact of Inflation on Private Pensions" (Paper presented at the Southern Economic Meetings, Washington, D.C., 1978).

6. Thomas R. Hoffman, "Retirement Funding: Impact of Inflation and Interest Rates" (Paper presented at the twenty-fourth international meeting of the Institute of Management Science, Honolulu, June 1979).

7. For an elaboration of the complexities involved, see Glenn D. Allison and Howard E. Winklevoss, *Transactions of the Society of Actuaries*, vol. 27 (1975), pp. 197–209.

3

Capital Asset Markets
and Inflation

This chapter reviews recent research on investment returns from security investments during inflationary periods and examines the performance of capital asset markets in general. In chapter 4 we consider the experience of individual pension funds.

Investment Returns and Inflation

The conventional wisdom before and during the 1960s maintained that capital market returns, particularly returns on holdings of common stock, would keep pace with inflation. Indeed, in the U.S. experience, there was no evidence to contradict this assumption. Annual real returns on equities, bonds, and short-term debt instruments during the period 1926–1968 tended to be overwhelmingly positive. (See table 6, which shows the annual real rates of return that would have been experienced by an investor who bought at the beginning of the indicated period and sold at the end.) If this experience had continued, pension funds would have remained solvent and would not have required their corporate sponsors to make unexpectedly large contributions to meet their obligations under inflationary conditions. Pension fund assets would have continued to grow in line with pension liabilities (which, we should recall, tend to grow with wages). Indeed, if security market returns consistently kept pace with inflation, corporate sponsors could even seriously contemplate the idea of indexing pension benefits. Unfortunately, the experience of the late 1960s and 1970s has contradicted conventional wisdom.

Stock returns have not kept pace with inflation: after a decade—1960 to 1969—that witnessed a total compound annual real rate of return (dividends plus capital gains) on common stocks of roughly 6.8 percent, total real returns from common stocks, compounded annually over the period 1970–1979, approximated –2.1 percent, undoubtedly confounding pension fund planners. In the past decade fixed-

TABLE 6

ANNUAL COMPOUND REAL RATES OF RETURN ON INVESTMENTS, 1926–1978
(percent)

Years	Common Stocks			Corporate Bonds	Long-Term U.S. Government Bonds	U.S. Treasury Bills
1926–1929	19.2 –	(–1.1) =	20.3	6.3	6.1	4.7
1930–1934	–9.9 –	(–4.8) =	–5.1	12.9	9.7	5.8
1935–1939	10.9 –	0.8 =	10.1	5.0	4.0	–0.7
1940–1944	7.7 –	5.0 =	2.7	–1.7	–2.0	–4.8
1945–1949	10.7 –	5.8 =	4.9	–3.6	–2.3	–5.2
1950–1954	23.9 –	2.5 =	21.4	–0.2	–0.9	–1.1
1955–1959	15.0 –	1.9 =	13.1	–2.2	–3.6	0.4
1960–1964	10.7 –	1.2 =	9.5	4.5	4.0	1.6
1965–1969	5.0 –	3.8 =	1.2	–6.0	–5.9	1.1
1970–1974	–2.4 –	6.6 =	–9.0	0.1	0.1	–0.7
1975–1978	13.9 –	6.9 =	7.0	1.5	–1.2	–1.1

NOTE: The table reflects the compound annual nominal total return on the instrument minus the compound increase in the consumer price index over the period. Each computation assumes purchase at the beginning of the period, sale at the end of the period, and reinvestment of dividends, interest, and, for treasury bills, proceeds when these are paid.

SOURCE: Roger G. Ibbotson and Rex A. Sinquefield, *Stocks, Bonds, Bills, and Inflation: Historical Returns (1926–1978)* (Charlottesville, Va.: Financial Analysts Research Foundation, 1979).

income investments did somewhat better than common stocks in keeping pace with inflation, although fixed-income securities have historically provided real returns generally below those of common stocks.[1]

A large amount of evidence shows that nominal monthly returns on broadly diversified portfolios of New York Stock Exchange common stocks were negatively correlated with inflation, as measured by the consumer price index (CPI), from the early 1950s through the mid-1970s.[2] Moreover, returns on common stocks responded negatively not only to the expected but also to the unexpected component of inflation. G. William Schwert shows this; it is especially surprising.[3]

The relation of stock returns to the consumer price index may not, of course, reveal the real performance of the firms whose equity is publicly held in the face of inflation. The relation does indicate, however, whether investors' purchasing power is preserved through equity investments.

One part of the logic underlying the notion that common stocks are a good inflation hedge derives from the observation that corporations' cash flows tend to move with inflation, though not perfectly. As the price level rises, corporate cash flows—revenue less costs less tax payments—should also rise. Another part of the logic supporting the view that common stocks are a good inflation hedge focuses on the fact that corporations tend to be financed with both equity and debt. If inflation increases unexpectedly, the interest payments to debt holders—which reflect only the anticipated component of inflation at the time debt was issued—remain fixed in nominal terms, thus reducing the real and market value of outstanding debt. Because debt holders receive no compensation for unanticipated inflation, shareholders ought to benefit from unexpected inflation at the expense of debt holders, provided the firm's monetary liabilities exceed its monetary assets.[4] Results for periods before the 1960s confirmed this hypothesis. Data drawn from the late 1960s and early 1970s, however, do not support the hypothesis.[5] Stockholders do not gain, at least to any measurable extent, at the expense of bondholders as a consequence of unexpected inflation. Recent experience suggests that both sets of investors lose to inflation.

Work by Fama and Schwert,[6] updated by Ibbotson and Fall,[7] shows that holders of fixed-income securities generally fared satisfactorily from 1970 to 1978. Although neither set of researchers offers substantive reasons for this finding, both show that investors in long-term corporate and government bonds and in short-term treasury bills by and large experienced returns that kept pace with inflation. (See table 6, for instance.) In this period, debt holders were not as grievously injured by inflation as investors in common stocks seem to have been. This result pertains only to the recent past, however. Typically, investors in bonds have lost whenever long-term interest rates have risen unexpectedly.

Even more damning evidence of the failure of common stocks as an inflation hedge comes from recent work by G. William Schwert.[8] He showed that stock prices tend to decline on the day that the unexpected component of the most recent monthly inflation rate (CPI) is announced. When the reported rate exceeds the expectation of the market, stock prices decline. When the actual rate is lower than the expectation, the market responds favorably.[9] This work shows that investors respond quickly and negatively to inflation because they are not pleased by high inflation. Although daily movements in stock prices may not be very revealing, the study does suggest that inflation is viewed unfavorably by investors, presumably because they no longer feel that common stocks provide the inflation hedge that the conventional wisdom led them to expect. The reason seems to be that inflation ultimately leads to reduced after-tax real rates of return for corporations and for their investors.[10]

Apart from common stocks and fixed-income securities, investors could hold other categories of assets. Fama and Schwert show that private residential real estate was a perfect hedge against inflation for 1953–1971, the period studied.[11] Ibbotson and Fall show that inflation strongly increased investment returns on both farms and housing.[12] In addition, Bodie has shown that portfolios of treasury bills hedged against unanticipated inflation with commodity futures contracts can provide a complete hedge against inflation.[13] Some brief analysis of these investment vehicles seems worthwhile in view of the increasing attention they are drawing.

Rates of return on real estate investments have kept pace with—indeed, have far exceeded—inflation, partly because of the many desirable tax benefits associated with such investments.[14] In a period of rapidly rising inflation and a rigid, nonindexed tax system, the relative desirability of real estate investments, which are accorded more favorable tax treatment than many other common forms of investment, is enhanced. Accordingly, one would expect to see bidding-up of real estate prices. The rapid appreciation might result, however, from a bidding-up of the values of the tax shields associated with real estate holdings rather than from an increase in the basic value of property.

It is not necessary to develop a formal model to see how tax shield values may be bid up: a simple numerical illustration suffices. The Hein and Lamb study provides data indicating that average mortgage rates were 5.81 percent in 1965 and 13.73 percent in 1980.[15] Interest payments are tax deductible, and the marginal tax bracket for a median income earner in 1965 ($7,610) was 17 percent, whereas for a median income earner in 1980 ($21,500) it was 24 percent. The after-tax cost of mortgage debt in 1965 was 5.81 (1 − 0.17), or 4.82 percent. In 1980 it was 10.4 percent. If inflation (or the rate of price appreciation for a house) was forecast at 2 percent in 1965, the real after-tax interest rate was 4.82 minus 2.0, or 2.82. In 1980, if inflation or the rate of house price appreciation was forecast at 8.0 percent, the real after-tax interest rate was 10.4 minus 8.0, or 2.4 percent, less than it was in 1965. This difference in real financing charges can be incorporated into housing prices, and it has been. Table 7 shows the change in housing prices and the change in the personal consumption deflator for 1965–1980. In nearly every year, housing prices have risen by more than the "inflation rate." This effect holds both for owner-occupied

TABLE 7

ANNUAL CHANGES IN HOUSING PRICES AND IN PERSONAL CONSUMPTION
DEFLATOR, 1965–1980
(percent)

Year	Housing Prices	Personal Consumption Deflator
1965	2.9	1.7
1966	3.5	2.9
1967	3.6	2.4
1968	5.6	4.1
1969	8.0	4.5
1970	3.0	4.7
1971	5.2	4.2
1972	6.4	3.7
1973	9.5	5.6
1974	9.3	10.1
1975	9.5	7.6
1976	8.6	5.2
1977	12.8	6.0
1978	13.7	6.8
1979	14.2	8.9
1980	10.1	10.2

SOURCE: Hein and Lamb, "Why the Median Priced Home Costs So Much," p. 12.

housing and for all other real estate and may be due to the bidding up of house prices in response to the decline in real financing costs.

The depreciation tax shield has provided an additional incentive for individuals and corporations to bid up the prices of residential and commercial real estate that is not owner occupied. Suppose that a warehouse purchased for $100,000 can be depreciated on a straight-line basis over twenty years. The annual tax shield equals the marginal tax rate of the investor times the annual depreciation. The higher the marginal tax rate, the more valuable is the tax shield. The "bracket creep" experienced in the United States during the past fifteen years as a consequence of inflation has raised marginal tax rates; so tax shields rise in value.

To continue the example, suppose, for simplicity, that the warehouse purchase was financed with equity. The value of the tax shield is, let us say, $5,000 per year times a 50 percent marginal tax rate, or $2,500 per year. Further suppose that the warehouse is rented for $5,000 per year. Rental income is offset by depreciation. At the end of ten years, the warehouse has a book value of $50,000. The combination of an inflation rate of 10 percent and a deterioration rate of 5 percent allows sale of the building for $162,100. The difference between the selling price and the book value is taxable at capital gains rates, let us say at 25 percent. The after-tax internal rate of return on this investment is 7.46 percent. This return involves no increase in rent. To duplicate this performance with a fully taxable instrument, say, a treasury bill with a return that is taxed at 50 percent, the pretax return would have to be 15.9 percent. The difference results from the fact that the warehouse investment allowed the owner to convert what would otherwise have been ordinary income to a capital gain. This privilege has value, and the greater the amount that can be so converted, the greater the value. Moreover, the warehouse could be financed with tax-advantaged debt, thus sweetening the later tax on equity.

These illustrations suggest that high and rising inflation coupled with a nonindexed tax system makes real estate increasingly attractive. If the inflation rate drops or if the tax system is indexed, however, real estate becomes less attractive. In the case of owner-occupied housing, if the 1980 marginal tax rate on income had been 17 percent, as it was in 1965, the real after-tax interest rate would have been 3.4 percent, not 2.4 percent. The higher real financing cost would result in a lower selling price for the house. Moreover, if inflation had been sufficiently low in the case of the warehouse that the selling price was $50,000, the internal rate of return would have been zero. A positive return would have required higher rent, and the amount in excess of depreciation would have been taxed at ordinary income tax rates. Inflation plays a role in permitting the conversion of ordinary income to capital gains.

We might also view these illustrations in a context of dynamic equilibrium. As nominal income rises when the tax system is not indexed to inflation, the value of tax shields—interest, depreciation, and the ability to convert ordinary income to capital gains—rises for any individual or organization. These shields are bid up in price. Once everyone is in the top marginal tax bracket, the shields are fully valued, and no extraordinary gains are likely to be associated with holding and reselling them.

Accompanying this logic, then, is an equilibrium distribution of real estate and associated tax-shield holdings among investors. As inflation pushes some investors into higher tax brackets, a new equilibrium distribution of the holding of tax shields ultimately emerges. When this equilibrium is reached, the future returns to real estate investment may fall, since all who need tax shields may already have them. It is not obvious, therefore, that real estate investments will be particularly germane to pension funds, that is, to tax-exempt investors, in the future. This is particularly likely to be the case if inflation falls or if marginal tax rates remain the same or fall.

Commodity futures contracts may be a fruitful investment alternative, but these markets tend to be quite risky (volatile), and they are somewhat thinner, that is, more subject to rapid price swings, than stock and bond markets are when large amounts are bought or sold. The relevant risk, of course, is the correlation of these contract values with other portfolio assets.[16] If the two are negatively correlated, then even though commodity futures contracts are themselves risky, adding them to a portfolio may reduce the riskiness of the portfolio. Nevertheless, it is not obvious that pension funds should base a significant portion of their portfolio strategy on their ability to make extensive use of commodity futures contracts. In view of these considerations, common stock and fixed-income-security markets seem the most relevant for pension funds.

The evidence shows that in the recent past real common stock returns have been negatively related to inflation, whereas the real returns on short-term government securities have at least been independent of inflation. The key question that must be addressed in the remainder of this chapter, therefore, is why returns in these markets, particularly in the stock market, have not kept pace with inflation. If we can learn why, then we are in a better position to confront the real issue, the identification of markets on which pension funds ought to concentrate. More specifically, we would like to know whether recent experience has been atypical or whether it merely foreshadows future developments.

If the negative relation between real returns on common stocks and inflation proves to be a mere statistical anomaly, there is no cause for concern. Investment strategies by which pension funds invest heavily in common stocks may be quite appropriate. If there is a more substantive explanation, however, of why common stock returns have been deficient in providing positive real returns in the face of inflation, it would be inappropriate for pension funds to follow the strategy of heavy investment in common stock unless the poor historical experience seemed likely to reverse itself. To anticipate our conclusions, we believe that the recent experience *has* been atypical and that there is a very real possibility that security markets will ultimately compensate investors for inflation. If investment policies followed by individual pension funds continue recent practices, however, they may be able to lose to inflation consistently, irrespective of how the aggregate markets behave.

The Stock Market and Inflation

In a recent empirical study, N. Bulent Gultekin explores expectations of experts regarding stock market returns and expected inflation.[17] Using data provided by "expert" forecasters, prominent economists, businessmen, and security analysts and collected by Joseph A. Livingstone, an economic journalist for the *Philadelphia Inquirer*, during the period June 1952 through December 1979, Gultekin examined the relationship between expected real returns on common stocks and expected inflation. In general, the higher the expected inflation, the higher were the expected real returns. Nominal common stock returns were expected to compensate not only for inflation but for inflation risk by providing for higher real returns than would be anticipated in a noninflationary environment. In short, the members of this panel of experts, and many other observers for that matter, expected a new trend that has not occurred. Indeed, these expectations reflect what Dr. Johnson once called "a triumph of hope over experience." The question is, Why?

At least four alternative hypotheses can be advanced regarding the poor performance of the stock market during the recent inflation: (1) it has been a chance occurrence; that is, the direct negative relation between real common stock returns and inflation is a statistical anomaly; (2) real stock returns, as a consequence of other structural changes in the economy, would have been low or negative even in the absence of inflation; (3) the relation exists because changes in the inflation rate interact with the tax system, unleashing forces that really do reduce the value of common stocks; and (4) the negative relation is a function of misperceptions on the part of market participants. Each of these hypotheses will be examined in turn.

Statistical Phenomena. In a major paper Eugene Fama shows that when explanatory variables in addition to inflation are included in a time-series regression having economically sensible real indicators of aggregate activity as independent variables and stock market returns as the dependent variable, inflation loses its explanatory power.[18] For the period 1953–1977, his evidence shows that real stock returns relate positively to measures of real activity. The measures of real activity are capital expenditures, real rates of return on nonfinancial corporate capital, and industrial production. Fama found that the empirical results negatively linking real stock returns and inflation were not robust, in the sense that inflation itself was acting only as a proxy for anemic real activity.

Fama's results further show that measures of real economic activity themselves relate negatively to inflation. Indeed, the evidence for this negative statistical relation is quite compelling. On balance, his research suggests that although the negative relation between real stock returns and inflation is a statistical anomaly, it is so only because inflation is a negative proxy for real economic activity. Moreover, changes in real economic activity may cause inflation, holding money growth constant. Milton Friedman subscribes to the general proposition that inflation and real activity growth are causally related but believes that causation runs from inflation to real activity.[19] If Fama's view of the causal relation is true, common stock prices will rise with an increase in real activity. If Friedman is right, common stock returns may inadequately compensate investors for losses in purchasing power during inflationary periods in that real activity will be deleteriously affected by inflation.

Some light is shed on this issue indirectly by Gultekin.[20] He examines the relation between real common stock returns and inflation in twenty-six countries for the period January 1947 through December 1979. Many of these countries have had substantially higher average inflation rates than the United States. We might be able to determine from an examination of Gultekin's conclusions whether the deleterious effects of inflation on real activity (or vice versa, hence on stock returns) are likely to disappear.

Unfortunately, Gultekin's results are not encouraging. For nineteen of twenty-six countries, he finds that real common stock returns have been negatively related to inflation. By examining a cross section, he shows that countries with higher inflation rates tend to enjoy higher nominal stock returns; but this is cold comfort, since real returns may be lower. Moreover, there seems to be no systematic way to characterize those seven countries in which stock returns were not adversely affected by inflation. These countries are Austria, France, Israel, Norway, Peru, Sweden, and the United Kingdom—nations that, superficially at least, have few economic common denominators. Gultekin does not construct a portfolio of international securities and relate the returns on that portfolio to "world" inflation, but such an experiment would very likely only confirm prior results.

Gultekin does not examine any country in detail comparable to that in Fama's analysis of the United States; however, it is certainly plausible to assume that inflation may have played the same proxy role in these countries that it did in the United States. If real economic activity—which drives stock prices—is negatively related to inflation, then inflation and stock returns are negatively related.

Related research by Dennis E. Logue and Richard James Sweeney shows a connection between high average inflation rates and high variability in real output growth.[21] They examined a cross section of countries from 1953 to 1971, comparing mean inflation rates and the variance in inflation rates with average real growth and its variability. Their findings combined with Gultekin's result support the belief that inflation and real activity are negatively related. Logue and Sweeney also show, however, that inflation seemingly has no relation to the average real increase in economic growth. Inflation seems to be related to variability in real growth, but it is not associated with a persistently lower growth rate. An economy will not necessarily, however, be achieving the level of economic activity of which it is capable. Indeed, persistent high inflation may relate to persistently low levels of economic output in relation to potential without being connected to the growth *rate*. It is possible to have a permanently lower *level* of economic activity than might otherwise be the case with no inflation. The growth rate could be unaffected, but the gap between potential and actual output could be large.

Fama's results dealt with a single country that has undergone a substantial increase in its inflation rate during the period of observation. His data may have reflected the initial downward shift in economic activity rather than a permanent deleterious relation between the rate of change in economic activity and inflation. Gultekin's evidence, in contrast, shows a negative relation across countries, presumably minimizing the effect of any single country's shift downward in the level of economic activity. There is possibly an alternative explanation, specifically, that inflation itself keeps the economy at less than full employment and hence results in a negative relation between inflation and stock returns. The question certainly begs for further research, since it is quite important for us to determine whether inflation has a once-and-for-all effect on the level of economic activity or whether it persistently reduces the real growth rate—or, indeed, whether inflation itself is caused by low rates of economic growth.

If inflation has a once-and-for-all effect on the level of economic activity but no persistent effect on a country's average real growth rate, then common stocks may perform considerably better in the future than in the past, even if the inflationary problem persists. If the effect of inflation on the real growth rate is persistent, however, common stocks may not provide real returns consistent with the assumptions made by corporations in planning their contributions to their pension funds, in which case changes are necessary.

Other Economic Changes. Michael Jensen and William Meckling argue that the U.S. government slowly began to erode the property rights of individuals and corporations with the New Deal of the 1930s and, at an accelerated pace, with the Great Society of the 1960s.[22] This usurpation of property rights, rather than any macroeconomic phenomenon, they contend, has been the principal culprit in causing stock prices to decline in real terms between the mid-1960s and the late 1970s. They cite as examples government involvement in curtailing the legal rights of bondholders in Penn Central as well as numerous programs that inhibit discretion on the part of investors and managers.

As it turns out, the erosion of property rights has been accompanied by the comparatively poor national economic performance attributed by others to inflation. Lower rates of investment, real output growth, and profitability may not have been a consequence of inflation at all. Instead, they may have resulted from the erosion of a person's or a firm's ability to use capital in any ethical way: the usurpation of property rights coincided with more rapid inflation. Certainly, once any government is willing to rearrange the existing structure of property rights, the likelihood of its willingness to debase the currency must be high.

This insight can be blended with several others regarding real economic growth and inflation to form an interesting, though highly speculative, hypothesis. We might identify as a starting point an erosion in property rights in consequence of which real economic activity slows. The government tries to stimulate the economy, to encourage economic growth, with its customary monetary and fiscal tools and perhaps through further erosions of property rights, such as special credit programs. This action causes inflation and further reductions in real output. Stock returns, of course, fail to keep pace with inflation, not because of inflation per se but because of the slowdown in economic activity that may precede it and certainly accompanies it.

Inflation, Taxes, and Stock Prices. Martin Feldstein and Huston McCulloch have developed a theory that purports to show why share prices will fall with an increase in the inflation rate.[23] At steady rates of inflation, share prices will rise, generally providing a positive real rate of return. If the average rate of inflation increases, however, share prices will fall, at least until a new equilibrium is reached. Then share prices will continue to rise at the usual rate.

Feldstein argues that current U.S. tax rules result in lower corporate valuations when inflation rises from one rate to another. He states: "The higher effective rate of tax on corporate income caused by historic-cost depreciation and the tax on artificial capital gains caused by inflation both reduce the real net yield that investors receive per unit of capital."[24]

25

He further suggests reasons why stock prices have not kept pace with inflation that are comparatively consistent with Fama's notions: real rates of economic growth, he argues, are hampered by the higher effective tax rates.

If Feldstein's conjectures are correct, investors in common stocks, including pension funds, hope that if the higher rate of inflation achieved in the late 1970s does not increase further—that is, if a steady state is achieved or if the rate of inflation declines—stock prices may provide a hedge against steady inflation.

McCulloch's view is much the same:

> Because the income tax is based on current dollar accounting, inflation turns the income tax into a tax on capital. Part of what should be figured as capital turns up as income in the accounts, and is taxed just as if it were true profit income. Consequently, if the tax rate and the inflation rate are sufficiently high compared to the real rate of return on capital the real rate of return after tax may actually be negative. Once this happens, there will be no further incentive to invest. Hoarding consumer goods will at least give a zero real rate of return, so why buy corporate stock? Savings will dry up and the real capital stock of the nation will dwindle as existing capital equipment depreciates.[25]

Again, in this view salvation lies either in reduced inflation or in a tax system that directly compensates for the effect of inflation on real after-tax returns.

Misperceptions. Alas, the possibility that inflation has no effect on real economic activity and hence no persistent influence on real market return remains, albeit just barely. If, indeed, there is no connection between real activity and inflation, then the principal effect of inflation may have been to confuse investors. Inflation may simply have made corporate security valuation more difficult and so may have led investors to set "inappropriate" security values. Although this idea conflicts with the vast accumulation of empirical evidence supporting the notion of rational expectations and security market efficiency, it remains a possibility.[26] Inflation may have prompted investors systematically to undervalue the real earnings of corporations. If this is the case, of course, pension fund investors (and any sort of investor) would do well to set an investment strategy heavily skewed toward common stock investments: sooner or later the market as a whole will come to its senses.

Franco Modigliani and Richard A. Cohn are the chief proponents of this view. They argue that investors make two major errors in evaluating common stocks:

> First, in inflationary periods, investors capitalize equity earnings at a rate that parallels the nominal interest rate, rather than the economically correct rate—the nominal rate less the inflation premium. In the presence of inflation, one properly compares the cash return on stocks, not with the nominal return on bonds, but with the real return on bonds.
>
> Second, investors fail to allow for the gain to shareholders accruing from depreciation in the real value of nominal corporate liabilities. . . .
>
> Rationally valued, the level of the S&P 500 at the end of 1977 should have been 200. Its actual at that time was 100. Because of inflation-induced errors, investors have systematically undervalued the stock market by nearly 50 percent.[27]

Commentary on this view is difficult, if not impossible. Most people are not comfortable, however, with the notion of misperceptions that last for years. Indeed, the Gultekin analysis of expectational data suggests that such misperceptions are not possible.[28] To accept the idea that investors persistently misperceive the effect of inflation while observing that informed investors correctly expect rising stock prices in the face of inflation seems to be quite illogical. If all other things were the same, these same investors would be bidding up the prices of common stock, thus leading to a fulfillment of their expectations.

If the Modigliani-Cohn hypothesis is correct, it holds the promise that once the misperceptions have disappeared, stock prices will experience explosive growth. Then real common stock returns will compensate not only for current inflation but also for past inflation.

Conclusion

In chapter 2 we saw how inflation could erode the real value of pension funds. Offsetting this phenomenon are security market returns that keep pace with inflation. If nominal returns rose with the inflation rate, thus allowing for positive real investment returns, pension funds would not be harmed by inflation.

Unfortunately, the evidence shows that in recent years stock market returns have not kept pace with inflation. In fact, real returns on common stock investments have been negatively correlated with inflation. Real returns on short-term fixed-income securities have tended to be substantially less adversely affected. Real returns on real estate and commodity futures not only have been unaffected by inflation but may in fact have benefited from it.

This chapter has also explored reasons for the failure of nominal stock returns to keep pace with inflation. Of the possibilities, only one is very optimistic. At some point investors' misperceptions must fade. The alternative explanations are more likely to be correct but may be less enthralling to anyone who confidently forecasts a continuation of or perhaps an increase in the inflation rate. Under the third hypothesis, stock returns will keep pace with inflation or will exceed inflation once inflation achieves a steady state or declines. After-tax real rates of return on corporate assets will improve, and the tax on capital will tend to disappear. Under the first hypothesis, there is the chance that real economic activity either will experience a permanently lower growth rate or will at least be more variable. Since it is real economic activity—productivity growth, investment, and output—that drives stock prices (not inflation, at least not directly), only if real activity growth rises will real common stock returns be sufficiently large to permit corporations to meet their pension obligations without substantially increasing their rate of contribution to their pension funds. Similarly, if the erosion of property rights, not inflation, led to poor national economic performance, once that erosion is brought under control, future security market returns may improve upon their recent showing.

It is important to note, however, that none of the explanations for poor security market performance in the face of inflation suggests that the experience of the 1970s was typical. To the extent that inflation is brought under control at a low and steady rate, nothing inherent in the security price formation process would lead one to believe that security prices will not keep pace with inflation in the future. In addition, modifications of the tax system could help reduce the damaging influence of inflation on after-tax real returns.

We have now reviewed the inflation performance of security markets as a whole, which could be very different from the inflation performance of individual pension funds. Perhaps pension funds were able to do better than the markets in general. Perhaps pension funds were able to achieve positive real returns on their investment portfolios through astute security selection or through astute movements of funds among the various relevant markets. Evidence reported in chapters 4 and 5 suggests the opposite. In the next chapter, we will see how pension funds actually did do in the high-inflation environment of the 1970s.

Notes

1. See, for instance, table 6. Total nominal compound annual returns include, for stocks, dividends plus capital gains or losses; for bonds, they include coupon payments plus capital gains and losses. To put these in real terms, the nominal returns were deflated by the GNP price deflator. The formula begins with a return measure:

$$R_t = \frac{P_t + D_t}{P_{t-1}} - 1$$

where R_t is the return for period t, P_t is the price at the end of period t, P_{t-1} is the price at the end of the prior period, and D_t is the dividend payment during period t. To measure real returns, deflate:

$$1 + RR_t = \frac{1 + R_t}{1 + \text{GNP price deflator}}$$

For annual compound real returns:

$$RR_{\text{for period}} = \left[\prod_{t=1}^{T} (1 + RR_t) \right]^{1/T} - 1$$

2. See, for example, Zvi Bodie, "Common Stocks as a Hedge against Inflation," *Journal of Finance*, vol. 31 (May 1976), pp. 459–70; Eugene F. Fama and G. William Schwert, "Asset Returns and Inflation," *Journal of Financial Economics*, vol. 5 (November 1977), pp. 115–46; Jeffrey Jaffe and Gershon Madelker, "The Fisher Effect for Risky Assets: An Empirical Investigation," *Journal of Finance*, vol. 31 (May 1976), pp. 447–58; and Charles R. Nelson, "Inflation and Rates of Return on Common Stock," *Journal of Finance*, vol. 31 (May 1976), pp. 471–83.

3. G. William Schwert, "The Adjustment of Stock Prices to Information about Inflation," *Journal of Finance*, vol. 36 (March 1981), pp. 15–29.

4. For a fuller elaboration and rudimentary tests of this hypothesis, see Armen Alchian and Reuben Kessel, "Redistribution of Wealth through Inflation," *Science*, vol. 130 (September 1959), pp. 535–39; George Bach and J. B. Stephenson, "Inflation and the Redistribution of Wealth," *Review of Economics and Statistics*, vol. 56 (February 1974), pp. 1–13; and Reuben Kessel and Armen Alchian, "Effects of Inflation," *Journal of Political Economy*, vol. 70 (December 1962), pp. 521–37.

5. Hai Hong, "Inflation and the Market Value of the Firm: Theory and Tests," *Journal of Finance*, vol. 32 (September 1977), pp. 1031–48.

6. Fama and Schwert, "Asset Returns and Inflation."

7. Roger G. Ibbotson and Carol L. Fall, "The United States Market Wealth Portfolio," *Journal of Portfolio Management* (Fall 1979), pp. 82–92.

8. Schwert, "Adjustment of Stock Prices."

9. Unexpected inflation is measured as the actual inflation rate less the nominal interest rate on short-term treasury bills that prevailed at the beginning of the period plus the expected real rate of interest. See Schwert, "Adjustment of Stock Prices," for elaboration on the merits of this measure.

10. Huston McCulloch, *Money and Inflation* (New York: Academic Press, 1975), shows that real after-tax returns to investors are reduced through inflation. Taxes are paid on the inflation rate as well as on the real rate of return. Similarly, for corporations with depreciation schedules set on the basis of historical cost, real tax payments rise with inflation, and after-tax real returns must fall.

11. Fama and Schwert, "Asset Returns and Inflation."

12. Ibbotson and Fall, "United States Market Wealth Portfolio."

13. Zvi Bodie, "An Innovation for Stable Real Retirement Income," *Journal of Portfolio Management* (Fall 1980), pp. 5-13.

14. For an illustration regarding residential property that also pertains to other real estate, see Scott E. Hein and James C. Lamb, Jr., "Why the Median Priced Home Costs So Much," *Federal Reserve Bank of St. Louis Review*, vol. 63, no. 6 (June/July 1981), pp. 11-20.

15. Ibid., p. 11.

16. Bodie, "An Innovation."

17. N. Bulent Gultekin, "Stock Market Returns and Inflation Forecasts: Test of Fisher Hypothesis with Expectations Data," Working paper (Chicago: University of Chicago, Graduate School of Business, 1981).

18. Eugene F. Fama, "Stock Returns, Real Activity, Inflation, and Money," *American Economic Review*, vol. 71 (September 1981), pp. 545-65.

19. Milton Friedman, "Nobel Lecture: Inflation and Unemployment," *Journal of Political Economy*, vol. 35 (June 1977), pp. 451-72.

20. N. Bulent Gultekin, "Stock Market Returns and Inflation: Evidence from Other Countries," Working paper (Hanover, N.H.: Dartmouth College, Amos Tuck School of Business Administration, 1980).

21. Dennis E. Logue and Richard James Sweeney, "Inflation and Real Growth: Some Empirical Evidence," *Journal of Money, Credit, and Banking* (November 1981), pp. 497-501.

22. Michael C. Jensen and William H. Meckling, *Can the Corporation Survive?* Reprint no. 6 (Los Angeles, Calif.: International Institute for Economic Research, 1977).

23. Martin Feldstein, "Inflation and the Stock Market," *American Economic Review*, vol. 70 (December 1980), pp. 839-47; and McCulloch, *Money and Inflation*, pp. 104-7.

24. Feldstein, "Inflation," p. 846.

25. McCulloch, *Money and Inflation*, p. 105.

26. For a summary of much work on this topic, see William F. Sharpe, *Investments*, 2d ed. (Englewood Cliffs, N.J.: Prentice-Hall, 1981).

27. Franco Modigliani and Richard A. Cohn, "Inflation, Rational Valuation, and the Market," *Financial Analysts Journal* (March/April 1979), pp. 24-44.

28. Gultekin, "Stock Market Returns and Inflation Forecasts."

4

Actual Performance of Pension Funds

This chapter examines the performance of 119 pension funds over five years, from the first quarter of 1974 until the fourth quarter of 1978. Managing pension funds was difficult in this volatile economic period. The main conclusion of this analysis is that decisions to change the funds' investment strategies in this period led to inferior performance. Only 5 or 6 of 119 pension funds were able to keep pace with inflation.

The first section of this chapter explains the data base and the calculations of returns. There follows an analysis of the rates of return and the portfolio mix of the funds, including a discussion of the total risk of the pension funds. The next section examines the beta risk of these pension funds as derived from regression work. Finally, we consider how the funds fared in relation to inflation.

A Description of the Data

All data were obtained from a large investment house in New York.[1] The data consist of the quarterly asset values, the cash flows, and the portfolio mix for 119 pension funds. The data are continuous from the fourth quarter of 1973 until the fourth quarter of 1978. The investment house began collecting data on these pension funds in 1973, and the fourth quarter of 1978 was the last date for which data were available when this study began. Market values of the individual funds at the end of 1978 ranged as high as $3.5 billion.

Table 8 presents the geometric mean of the monthly compounded quarterly total returns for each of the 119 pension funds in ranked order. The geometric mean is based on twenty quarterly observations per fund. The pension funds are assigned to portfolios in each of ten deciles, depending on the return performance of the funds. Nine portfolios contain twelve funds, and one contains eleven. The first-decile portfolio contains the funds with the lowest-ranked perform-

TABLE 8

AVERAGE QUARTERLY TOTAL RETURN FOR 119 PENSION FUNDS, IN RANKED ORDER

Rank within Decile	Decile Portfolio									
	1	2	3	4	5	6	7	8	9	10
1 (low)	−1.019	0.316	0.632	0.813	0.945	1.071	1.172	1.321	1.556	1.791
2	−0.602	0.365	0.662	0.833	0.947	1.072	1.181	1.324	1.605	1.800
3	−0.370	0.435	0.695	0.840	0.971	1.096	1.189	1.327	1.606	1.811
4	−0.298	0.463	0.703	0.842	1.005	1.102	1.194	1.347	1.619	1.851
5	−0.197	0.476	0.706	0.851	1.010	1.106	1.196	1.383	1.624	1.884
6	−0.166	0.508	0.723	0.852	1.011	1.107	1.233	1.424	1.630	1.885
7	−0.146	0.511	0.744	0.910	1.025	1.109	1.236	1.462	1.654	1.900
8	0.047	0.530	0.755	0.925	1.037	1.109	1.289	1.479	1.668	2.063
9	0.053	0.546	0.766	0.925	1.038	1.114	1.296	1.510	1.691	2.108
10	0.247	0.583	0.778	0.931	1.047	1.122	1.299	1.540	1.698	2.125
11	0.281	0.621	0.805	0.939	1.066	1.150	1.313	1.545	1.751	3.022
12 (high)	—	0.623	0.811	0.942	1.068	1.171	1.315	1.548	1.770	3.187

NOTE: These geometric returns are multiplied by 100 for expression as percentages.
SOURCE: Authors.

TABLE 9

AVERAGE QUARTERLY TOTAL RETURN AND STANDARD DEVIATION FOR 119 PENSION FUNDS, BY DECILE

Decile Portfolio	Geometric Mean (1)	Arithmetic Mean (2)	Standard Deviation (3)	Reward-to-Variability Ratio (4)
1	0.045	0.381	8.20	0.0465
2	0.462	0.809	8.37	0.0967
3	0.699	0.983	7.62	0.1290
4	0.913	1.172	7.30	0.1605
5	0.911	1.191	7.60	0.1567
6	1.046	1.290	7.09	0.1819
7	1.197	1.415	6.72	0.2106
8	1.234	1.421	6.21	0.2288
9	1.573	1.729	5.72	0.3023
10	2.246	2.400	5.69	0.4218

NOTE: The reward-to-variability ratio is column 2 divided by column 3.
SOURCE: Authors.

ance (based on the geometric mean) while the funds in decile portfolio 10 had the best performance. As shown in the table, the lowest performance is − 1.019 percent per quarter, and the highest is 3.187 percent per quarter. Only the five best-performing pension funds experienced total returns in excess of the average quarterly consumer price index. That is, only the last five funds achieved a positive average real rate of return during the mid-1970s.

Averages and deviations for the decile portfolios are given in table 9. Columns 1 and 2 list the geometric and arithmetic mean returns. The standard deviation around the arithmetic mean is given in column 3. The reward-to-variability ratio in column 4 is column 2 divided by column 3. As this table shows, the higher-decile portfolios had not only the highest average return but also the lowest total variability as measured by the standard deviations. The net result is reward-to-variability ratios that increase from the low-decile portfolios to the high-decile portfolios at a greater rate than the average returns. In other words, a rough adjustment for risk reveals that the high-decile portfolios performed even better than they appear to have performed when we consider returns alone.

The returns for each decile portfolio plotted quarter by quarter reveal a fairly similar pattern. Each decile portfolio has positive and negative returns at the same time. The feature that distinguishes the portfolios in different deciles is the magnitude of the quarterly return. A comparison of portfolio 10 and portfolio 1 shows that in quarters when both have positive returns, portfolio 10 does not consistently have a greater return than portfolio 1 but, in negative-return quarters, portfolio 1 usually does worse than portfolio 10.

Asset Mix, Timing, and Faulty Judgments

To determine why decile portfolio 1 recorded returns consistently lower than portfolio 10 in bad quarters yet did no better in good quarters, it is useful to examine the quarterly performance of several passive indexes of security market returns. The term "passive" simply refers to portfolios that seek to provide investment results that correspond to the price and yield performance of the index under consideration.

Table 10 presents eight such indexes. No adjustment is made for transaction costs. Column 1 is common stock return measured by the Standard and Poor's 500 index of common stocks; column 2 is the return on the Salomon Brothers' high-grade long-term corporate bond index; and column 3 is the ninety-day treasury bill rate. The index in column 4 is an equally weighted average of columns 1, 2, and 3. Column 5 lists the return on a portfolio containing 56.35 percent of stocks (column 1), 29.92 percent of bonds (column 2), and 13.73 percent of treasury bills (column 3). These percentages reflect the average portfolio mixture of the 119 pension funds during this period. The perfect foresight index in column 6 shows the return that would have been possible if a fund had timed the market perfectly each quarter by shifting into common stocks, bonds, or treasury bills.

Columns 7 and 8 show the quarterly changes in the consumer price index and the GNP deflator index. Approximate real quarterly returns can be obtained by subtracting column 7 or 8 from any of the returns in columns 1 to 6. At the bottom of the table are a geometric average, an arithmetic average, and the standard deviation of the quarterly returns. In addition, a reward-to-variability measure is provided by taking a ratio of the arithmetic mean to the standard deviation.

The return on the common stock index was positive in nine quarters and negative in eleven quarters, producing an average quarterly return of 1.07 percent over the five years. The common stock index also had the greatest return variability. Both the bond index and the treasury bill index had greater average returns and substantially less variability than the stock index. The equally weighted index did eight basis points better on average than the treasury bill index with about

34

half the variability of the stock index. The average-weighted index had more stocks and fewer treasury bills than an equally weighted index, resulting in about the same return yet more variability.

Returns in column 6 show that if there were a way to time market swings perfectly, managers of pension funds could have achieved spectacular returns on their investments. A fund that chose the right asset mixture each quarter would have earned an average quarterly return of 6.18 percent. Such a strategy would have meant investing in stocks for seven quarters, long-term bonds for four quarters, and treasury bills for nine quarters.

Table 11 lists the percentage of total assets in equity of the ten portfolio deciles and shows that the funds that maintained the most equity were on average the funds with the worst performance. This is only a partial explanation, however, of why decile 1 did so much worse than decile 10. Columns 2 to 4 in table 11 are very useful in answering the portfolio mixture question. The standard deviations in column 2 show that the funds that were most active in moving their assets between stocks and other investment vehicles did the worst. The best four performance deciles maintained a fairly consistent equity mixture in their portfolios. The apparent strategy of the better-performing funds was to keep approximately 50 percent of their funds in equities in both good and bad markets. The better-performing funds did not attempt to time the volatile swings of the stock market.

It is possible that there is a small bias in the numbers; because equities are volatile, portfolios with high percentages in equities have greater volatility than portfolios with lower percentages in equities. Thus they also have higher standard deviations in the percentage in equities, even without any movements by the managers. It can be argued, of course, that the manager should constantly change his asset mixture to keep the desired percentage in equities despite fluctuations in the market.

An examination of the changes in the percentage of total assets held in equities shows that decile 1, which had the poorest performance, was the most heavily invested in equities at the beginning of the period. Although the data are not shown, this portfolio mixture coincided with a deep decline in the stock market during 1974. It could be argued that if the funds included in decile 1 had not been as heavily invested in stocks at this time, their performance would have been much better. Although this statement is undoubtedly true, the conscious decision beginning in 1975 to reduce the emphasis on equities in decile 1 is the principal reason for its poor performance. Unfortunately for the funds that reduced their equities, the Standard and Poor's index from 1975 through 1978 actually had a relatively good

TABLE 10
Average Quarterly Total Return for Eight Passive Portfolios, 1974–1978

Quarter	Common stock (1)	Bond (2)	Treasury bill (3)	Equally weighted (4)	Average weighted (5)	Perfect foresight (6)	CPI (7)	GNP deflator (8)
1974								
First	-2.82	-3.51	1.78	-1.52	-2.39	1.78	3.33	2.11
Second	-7.56	-5.18	2.11	-3.54	-5.52	2.11	2.65	2.79
Third	-25.16	-3.07	2.12	-8.70	-14.81	2.12	3.26	2.90
Fourth	9.38	9.30	1.76	6.81	8.31	9.38	2.44	3.15
1975								
First	22.94	4.75	1.43	9.71	14.54	22.94	1.54	2.71
Second	15.37	3.60	1.30	6.76	9.92	15.37	1.78	1.44
Third	-10.95	-3.29	1.50	-4.25	-6.95	1.50	1.87	1.89
Fourth	8.65	9.23	1.46	6.45	7.84	9.23	1.65	1.51
1976								
First	14.97	4.22	1.21	6.80	9.86	14.97	0.72	1.01
Second	2.48	0.30	1.22	1.33	1.65	2.48	1.55	1.23
Third	-3.00	5.56	1.34	1.30	0.16	5.56	1.48	1.15
Fourth	3.14	7.52	1.21	3.96	4.19	7.52	0.99	1.36
1977								
First	-7.44	-2.32	1.09	-2.89	-4.74	1.09	2.22	1.27
Second	3.32	3.86	1.15	2.78	3.18	3.86	2.02	1.78
Third	-2.82	1.08	1.30	-0.15	-1.09	1.30	1.20	1.23

Passive Portfolio

Fourth	−0.13	−0.82	1.49	0.18	−0.11	1.49	1.14	1.58
1978								
First	−4.92	0.03	1.49	1.13	−2.56	1.49	1.93	1.63
Second	8.50	−1.09	1.60	3.00	4.68	8.50	2.95	2.61
Third	8.67	3.09	1.75	4.50	6.05	8.67	1.95	1.94
Fourth	−4.93	−2.06	2.18	−1.60	−3.10	2.18	1.91	2.46
Geometric mean	0.82	1.46	1.52	1.23	1.04	6.02	1.93	1.89
Arithmetic mean	1.38	1.56	1.52	1.60	1.55	6.18	1.93	1.89
Standard deviation	10.86	4.36	0.33	5.09	6.77	6.00	0.72	0.66
Reward-to-variability ratio	0.10	0.36	4.61	0.31	0.23	1.03	2.68	2.86

NOTES: The common stock index is the Standard and Poor's 500 index. The bond index is the Salomon Brothers' high-grade long-term corporate bond index. The treasury bill index is the return on a ninety-one-day treasury bill. The equally weighted portfolio contains one-third of the stock index, one-third of the bond index, and one-third of the treasury bill index. The average-weighted portfolio contains 56.35 percent stocks, 29.92 percent bonds, and 13.73 percent treasury bills. The perfect foresight index was formed by taking the best quarterly return of the stock, bond, and treasury bill index in each quarter. The CPI index contains the quarterly changes in the consumer price index. The GNP deflator is the gross national product price deflator. The reward-to-variability ratio is the ratio of the arithmetic mean to the standard deviation.
SOURCE: Authors.

TABLE 11

Average Percentage of Equity in Each Portfolio Decile and Its Standard Deviation, 119 Pension Funds, 1974–1978

Performance Decile	Average Equity (1)	Standard Deviation (2)	Minimum Percentage (3)	Maximum Percentage (4)
1	64.89	8.74	47.32	77.20
2	61.34	4.64	54.66	71.37
3	60.29	4.85	52.69	70.48
4	57.68	4.61	49.03	63.38
5	61.15	5.92	50.93	71.55
6	56.14	6.28	46.05	65.51
7	52.60	3.68	48.16	62.21
8	50.85	3.99	44.19	59.65
9	45.49	2.84	38.99	50.06
10	45.25	3.15	39.94	51.77
All funds	56.35	4.27	38.99	77.20

SOURCE: Authors.

total quarterly return of 2.97 percent. This rate of return was substantially better than the returns during this period from fixed-income instruments or treasury bills. If the funds in decile 1 had maintained a consistent emphasis on equities, they would have done considerably better.

The reason for decile 1's poor performance is that these funds attempted to move pension assets according to their judgment about how the different markets would perform. The market headed in a different direction once the funds in decile 1 had adjusted to meet the changes that they incorrectly anticipated. The market-timing decisions made by pension funds during this volatile period hurt their performance. It was not the emphasis on equities that harmed the funds in the lower-performing deciles but rather their decision to move assets away from equities at the wrong time.

The rates of return for the passive portfolios shown in table 10 may be compared with the average quarterly total returns for the pension funds shown in table 8. Standard and Poor's 500 geometric average was 0.8 percent, and 83 of the 119 funds were able to realize a return greater than this index. Yet only 27 funds were able to return more than the average rate of return on treasury bills (1.52 percent) during this period.

It is disturbing that only a small number of funds beat the average-weighted and equally weighted indexes shown in table 10. Only thirty-three funds were able to better the return on the average portfolio mixture. A mere twenty-eight funds did better than simply following the strategy of one-third stocks, one-third bonds, and one-third treasury bills. The poor performance is measured before management fees but after brokerage cost fees. The funds with substandard performance were also incurring risk for which they were not compensated. A passively managed portfolio that continuously held equal portions of stocks, bonds, and treasury bills would have performed better than the typical pension fund.

A comparison of the performance of the portfolio deciles with the performance of the passive indexes in table 10 in good and bad markets for the passive indexes showed that in an up market the deciles did about the same but, during periods of negative rates of return, there were sizable differences among the portfolio deciles. This finding also supports the conclusion that the portfolio managers in deciles in which assets were moved among markets made poor portfolio choices on the average.

Because of the devastating effect that losses have on compound returns, of course, it is not surprising that the funds with the best cumulative performance have avoided substantial losses during bad periods. This behavior is apart from the psychological response of managers suffering large losses, who frequently become more conservative before the market turns up.

Analysis of Beta Risk

This section presents the results of regressions between quarterly returns of the 119 pension funds and the quarterly returns of the eight indexes listed in table 10. Specifically, the following time-series regression is fitted using twenty quarterly returns:

$$R_{it} = \alpha_j + \beta_j I_{jt} + \text{error term}$$

where R_{it} is the return on pension fund i during quarter t and I_{jt} is the return on index j during quarter t. Coefficients α_j and β_j are obtained for each of the seven indexes.

The results of the regression analysis by the ten performance deciles are presented in table 12. The β_j coefficients measure the variability of pension fund returns in relation to the different passive index portfolios during the sample period.

The average beta coefficients β_j presented in table 12 suggest several interesting conclusions about the performance of the decile. First, the betas, or systematic risk measures, in columns 1–2 and 4–6 follow

TABLE 12
Average Betas Using Passive Portfolios, by Decile

Decile	Common Stock (1)	Bond (2)	Treasury Bill (3)	Equally Weighted (4)	Average Weighted (5)	Perfect Foresight (6)	CPI (7)
1 (low)	0.81	1.45	−11.00	1.64	1.28	1.16	−5.87
2	0.76	1.33	−10.56	1.55	1.21	1.11	−5.27
3	0.69	1.22	−10.19	1.42	1.10	1.01	−5.01
4	0.66	1.23	−9.49	1.35	1.06	0.98	−4.75
5	0.69	1.32	−10.22	1.43	1.11	1.03	−5.15
6	0.64	1.26	−10.05	1.34	1.04	0.96	−4.85
7	0.61	1.12	−8.95	1.26	0.98	0.92	−4.32
8	0.56	1.08	−8.96	1.16	0.91	0.83	−4.23
9	0.51	1.01	−8.35	1.06	0.83	0.79	−3.69
10 (high)	0.52	0.92	−7.03	1.04	0.83	0.81	−3.50

SOURCE: Authors.

40

the same pattern as the standard deviations of various market segments (total risk measures) presented in table 10. The better-performing deciles have the lower risk. The worst-performing deciles have acquired portfolios that are also riskier.

Column 5 in table 12 presents the average-weighted beta coefficient by decile. The betas in this column come close to estimating the volatility of the pension fund assets weighted by the average portfolio mixture of the 119 funds. Decile 1 had an average beta during this period of 1.28. Decile 10 had a much lower beta of 0.83.

According to modern portfolio theory, we would expect decile 1 to perform much worse than decile 10 in down markets.[2] As our ex post performance results illustrate, this is precisely what occurred. Modern portfolio theory would also suggest, however, that in rising markets decile 1 would do better than decile 10. As noted previously, we did not observe differing returns across deciles in good markets. The validity of the theory could then be questioned: Why did the funds not do better in "up" markets, as their betas suggest? The theory, however, is predicated on a mixture of assets that remains constant over time. If the mixture of stocks and bonds changed during the period, as it did, the theory has not been disproved. Therefore the changing composition of the portfolio resulted in suboptimal performance because in rising markets these funds were incorrectly positioned. The beta results are useful in further showing that the conscious decision to move assets hurt performance.

Table 13 presents the decile performance adjusted for beta risk. This table of risk-adjusted performance was calculated by dividing the beta in table 12 by the appropriate decile returns in table 8. Columns 1, 2, 5, and 6 of table 13 show that on a risk-adjusted basis the highest-return deciles also have the highest risk-adjusted performance. This beta risk measurement offers the same conclusion as the total risk adjustment measure in table 9. Essentially, the less market risk borne by a fund, the higher the rate of return. This inversion of the expected positive risk and return relation has been explained by the poor timing of the asset changes in the lower-performing deciles.

Inflation and Returns

The average quarterly inflation rate during this period as measured by the CPI index was 1.93 percent. Only 5 pension funds of the 119 in this study had a geometric average better than this inflation rate. Only 6 pension funds had a geometric return greater than the 1.89 percent quarterly rate of the GNP deflator. (See table 8.) By chance, at a 5 percent level we would expect about 6 funds to better the inflation

TABLE 13
Decile Performance Adjusted for Beta Risk

Performance Decile	Common Stock (1)	Bond (2)	Treasury Bill (3)	Equally Weighted (4)	Average Weighted (5)	Perfect Foresight (6)	CPI (7)
1	0.47	0.26	-0.035	0.23	0.30	0.33	-0.065
2	1.06	0.61	-0.077	0.52	0.67	0.73	-0.154
3	1.42	0.81	-0.096	0.69	0.89	0.97	-0.196
4	1.78	0.95	-0.123	0.87	1.11	1.20	-0.247
5	1.73	0.90	-0.117	0.83	1.07	1.16	-0.231
6	2.02	1.02	-0.128	0.96	1.24	1.34	-0.266
7	2.32	1.26	-0.158	1.12	1.44	1.54	-0.328
8	2.54	1.14	-0.159	1.23	1.56	1.71	-0.335
9	3.39	1.71	-0.207	1.63	2.08	2.19	-0.469
10	4.62	2.61	-0.341	2.31	2.89	2.96	-0.686

Source: Authors.

TABLE 14
CORRELATION OF INFLATION WITH TOTAL RETURNS

Performance Decile	Correlation
1	− 0.47
2	− 0.45
3	− 0.47
4	− 0.46
5	− 0.47
6	− 0.47
7	− 0.46
8	− 0.48
9	− 0.46
10	− 0.44

SOURCE: Authors.

rate. Therefore the hypothesis that the average pension fund return was statistically superior to the inflation rate can be rejected.

Table 14 presents the correlation of total quarterly returns with the CPI inflation rate over the entire period. The consistent negative correlations shown in this table imply that, as inflation rises, pension returns fall. Economic theory would posit that an unanticipated rise in the rate of inflation prevented the funds from keeping pace with inflation.

Columns 3 and 7 of table 12 present the betas of the treasury bill index and the consumer price index. Both indexes reflect the changing inflationary movement. Like the correlations in table 14, the negative betas imply that, as inflation rose, the returns on pension funds declined. The deciles with the lowest performance were more affected by inflation. The funds as a group did not cope well with the inflation of the 1970s.

Conclusion

The funds with the worst performance were those that moved assets among relevant security markets most frequently. The pension funds that followed a consistent strategy proved to be the best performers. When we adjust for risk, the difference in performance is even more striking. The analysis has illustrated that the inverse risk-and-reward relation is not at odds with investment theory. The high-beta deciles did worse in falling markets than the low-beta deciles. In rising markets high-beta deciles had incorrectly positioned assets because of their propensity to move funds. Specifically, the managers' propensity to move funds incorrectly, rather than the mere moving of funds, caused the problem. Finally, the inflation of the 1970s surpassed the returns on all but a few of the pension funds sampled.

Notes

1. Data on pension funds were provided by Arthur Williams III of Merrill, Lynch, Pierce, Fenner, and Smith. The data were supplied in a coded format in such a way that we were unable to link pension funds with sponsoring companies or investment managers.

2. According to modern portfolio theory, risk is best analyzed in a portfolio context. Portfolio risk can be measured by the variance or standard deviation of period-to-period returns. The variability of portfolio returns, however, is composed of market risk and unique risk. Unique risk can be diversified away by investors, but market risk cannot be avoided.

The capital asset pricing model posits expected returns on a security or portfolio that are linearly related to market risk as measured by beta. Beta measures the amount investors expect the portfolio value to change for each additional 1 percent change in the market. Thus beta is simply a measure of the sensitivity of a portfolio's return to market movements. The average beta of all securities is 1.0. A portfolio with a beta greater than 1.0 is more sensitive to market movements. A portfolio with a beta lower than 1.0 is less sensitive. Finally, the standard deviation of a well-diversified portfolio is proportional to beta.

5

One Company's Pension Fund: A Case Study

This chapter analyzes the investment performance of the pension fund of an anonymous large manufacturing corporation, company Y. Company Y is a member of the Fortune 500, with pension fund management problems similar to those of other U.S. corporations.[1] The available data are for the period 1970 to 1978. The aim of the analysis is to provide insights into the decision making of a typical pension fund.

The first section of this chapter examines the objectives and proposed tactics of company Y's pension fund. We then review the fund's performance and compare it with that of the financial markets and with that of other pension funds. The third section describes the decisions that led to the investment results. The chapter concludes by discussing actual performance in the context of the stated objectives and proposes strategies that might have yielded better performance.

The Fund's Objectives and Proposed Tactics

The basic goal of most major corporations for their pension fund is to achieve an investment performance that will guarantee pensioners adequate retirement benefits.[2] Increased rates of return will allow the corporation either to reduce its pension expenses or to increase benefits without increasing the amount of funding. Because higher expected rates of return may be accompanied by higher levels of risk, however, the corporation must balance the desire for better investment results with an appropriate level of volatility. In seeking a high rate of return, a pension fund has the advantage of having a long time horizon compared with that of most other investors because of the special nature of pension liabilities. A portion of the fund's assets can be held in riskier investments than are suitable for other investors because pension funds pay out benefits over a long period of time.

The specific goals of company Y's pension fund, based on the company's prior experience and expected needs, were safety, a targeted real rate of return, investment liquidity, and a targeted distribution of income between dividends and interest and capital appreciation. These goals reflect the desire to maximize returns, to take a long-term view of investments, and to reduce risk to a sensible level. In analyzing the fund's performance over the period 1970–1978, we may usefully keep in mind these objectives and the strategic actions they imply.

At the end of 1978, the pension fund's contributions and investment income exceeded its benefit payments by two to one. Although this wide difference implies that the pension fund could make investments having a fairly long payoff period, the corporation was concerned that during a period of economic failure there might be negative rates of return and a fall in the corporate cash flow from which contributions are made. As a result, the fund sought to maintain liquidity equal to 2.5 percent of its assets to ensure that the fund would be able to make two and one-half years of benefit payments. The fund sought an investment posture that would not overemphasize the long-term nature of its pension liabilities and would be sufficiently diverse to provide liquidity, safety, and potential growth.

The targeted rate of return for company Y was a 3–4 percent *real* return. Assuming a 7 percent inflation rate, the fund would have to earn 10 to 11 percent. This return objective was based on consultation with a major actuarial consulting firm and was expected to be sufficient to meet the benefit objectives of the fund as well as to reduce its actuarial unfunded liability.

To achieve this real return, the fund committed itself to what was considered an aggressive portfolio mixture. The term "aggressive," as defined by the fund, meant equity investment equal to 40 to 70 percent of the fund's assets. It was expected that investing in common stock would offset the damage done by inflation to the pension fund's overall worth. In regard to the management of the equity investment, the fund hired and retained money managers who had been in the upper half of the A. G. Becker universe during the previous three- to five-year period.[3] The objective of the equity investment was to equal or to better the return on the Standard and Poor's 500 common stock index. To achieve this goal, the fund sponsor concluded that growth stocks ought to be emphasized. This emphasis implied that the sponsor either wanted to hold a portfolio of securities with relatively high risk or believed that growth stocks were undervalued by the market at that time. If the reason for the emphasis on growth stocks was the former, this was the way the sponsor reconciled taking the higher risk with its desire for a higher expected return.

Although the fund planned to maintain an aggressive posture in equities, it also desired to maintain reasonable liquidity to take advantage of changing money-market conditions. As the investment climate changed, the fund planned to take advantage of new opportunities. It was expected that the large portion of assets committed to equities would provide the flexibility and liquidity necessary to alter investment strategy rapidly. At the end of 1978, the fund had 52 percent of its assets in common stock.

The fund's objective of maintaining sufficient liquidity indicates that the corporation officials believed that the pension managers had the ability to time market swings and therefore should pursue an active policy of altering the investment mixture. By correctly positioning pension assets before a major market change, the fund could, in principle, substantially improve its performance. In addition, because of the liquidity objective, it was not considered particularly desirable to include real estate in the portfolio. Traditionally, real estate has been considered less liquid than stocks or bonds and would therefore reduce the flexibility of the fund.

An additional goal of the fund concerned the method by which returns were to be realized—at least one-half of the expected annual return was to be in the form of cash dividends and interest; the remainder would come from capital appreciation. The strategy of realizing 50 percent of the fund's expected returns as current income competed with its other goal of emphasizing growth stocks, even though the company stated that dividends were actually relatively high on their growth stocks. It is usually difficult for growth companies to outperform the general growth of the economy unless they retain earnings for future expansion. The growth stocks included in company Y's portfolio were companies entering the mature phase of their life cycle. Historically, such companies have tended to make higher dividend payments. A pension policy of achieving a relatively high rate of return commensurate with volatility would probably require having a smaller portion of the return as current income and a larger portion as capital appreciation.

The fund's last substantive objective was to reduce the proportion of long-term bonds held. The corporation's officials believed that bonds with maturities longer than ten years were poor investments in periods of rapid inflation. This position implies the belief either that the bond market is incorrectly pricing such instruments or that the actual rate of inflation will exceed the expected inflation rate. If the latter were true, then the corporation officials would have made the right guess; if actual inflation proved less than expected, however, long-term bonds could be a good investment.[4]

Actual Performance of Company Y

Table 15 shows the annual total rates of return earned by the pension fund each year from 1970 to 1978. Table 16 shows the allocation of the assets in the fund. The compounded rate of return for company Y from 1970 to 1978 was 1.5 percent. Standard and Poor's index averaged a 4.5 percent return. Company Y did better than this index in only four of the nine years. This index had a higher level of total risk as measured by standard deviation, however. The reward-to-variability measure at the bottom of table 15 is a way of estimating risk-adjusted performance. This ratio is computed by dividing the arithmetic mean annual return for the 1970–1978 period by the standard deviation of the nine annual returns. The ratio tells us whether taking additional variability of return on average resulted in additional return. According to this ratio, Standard and Poor's index performed almost twice as well as company Y. There is a strong association between the company's return and Standard and Poor's index, the correlation coefficient being 0.95.

The performance of company Y's pension fund may be compared with those of other pension funds from 1974 through 1979 by using data on the 119 funds summarized in the previous chapter. The average annual return of the 119 funds was 4.2 percent. During the same period, company Y had an annual return of 0.74 percent. The fund would have ranked 105th of the 119 funds in this study. On a risk-adjusted basis, company Y's performance is also poor. The fund would have ranked somewhere in the middle of the second lowest decile. During the later 1970s, company Y made investment decisions that resulted in performance substantially lower than that of the typical pension fund.

From 1970 to 1978 the inflation rate outdistanced both the company's fund and the common stock index. Inflation was 5.2 percent higher per year than the rate of return earned on the pension assets of company Y. It is important to recognize that this period need not be characteristic of the relation between inflation and the return on equities generally. A study by Ibbotson and Sinquefield concluded that the real rate of return on common stocks during the fifty-three-year period 1926–1978 was 6.2 percent, compounded annually, and the rate of inflation over this period was 2.5 percent, compounded annually.[5]

TABLE 15

COMPARISON OF ANNUAL TOTAL RATES OF RETURN OF THE PENSION FUND OF COMPANY Y WITH OTHER RATES OF RETURN, 1970–1978

Year	Pension Fund of Company Y (1)	Common Stock Index (2)	Long-Term Corporate Bond Index (3)	Consumer Price Index (4)	GNP Deflator Index (5)
1970	−2.2	4.0	18.4	5.5	5.4
1971	16.2	14.3	11.0	3.4	5.0
1972	15.5	19.0	7.3	3.4	4.2
1973	−15.8	−14.7	1.1	8.8	5.7
1974	−24.5	−26.5	−3.1	12.2	8.7
1975	21.2	37.2	14.6	7.0	9.3
1976	9.6	23.8	18.6	4.8	5.2
1977	−3.5	−7.2	1.7	6.8	5.8
1978	7.2	6.6	−0.1	9.0	7.3
Geometric mean	1.5	4.5	7.5	6.7	6.3
Arithmetic mean	2.6	6.3	7.7	6.8	6.3
Standard deviation	15.4	19.9	8.3	2.9	1.7
Reward-to-variability ratio	0.17	0.32	0.93	2.34	3.70

NOTE: The common stock index is the Standard and Poor's 500 index. The bond index is the Salomon Brothers' high-grade long-term corporate bond index. The CPI index shows the annual changes in the consumer price index. The GNP deflator is the gross national product implicit price deflator. The reward-to-variability ratio is the ratio of the arithmetic mean to the standard deviation.
SOURCE: Authors.

TABLE 16
ALLOCATION OF THE PENSION FUND ASSETS OF COMPANY Y, BY MARKET VALUE, 1970–1978
(percent)

Year	Equities (1)	Fixed-Income Investments (2)	Real Estate (3)	Cash (4)
1970	68	6	22	4
1971	78	2	18	2
1972	82	2	13	3
1973	74	4	15	7
1974	60	11	18	11
1975	57	20	14	9
1976	59	16	0	25
1977	58	21	0	21
1978	52	15	0	33
Arithmetic mean	65.3	10.8	11.1	12.8
Standard deviation	10.6	7.6	8.7	11.0

SOURCE: Authors.

Although the short period from 1970 to 1978 appears to be a historic anomaly, it is useful to inquire why the return on company Y's pension fund was so far below the inflation rate.

A Year-by-Year Analysis of the Investment Decisions Made by Company Y

Tables 17, 18, and 19 may be used to analyze when and why the investment decisions of company Y's pension fund were made. Table 17 presents annual rates of return earned by the various portfolio managers employed by the fund; table 18 compares these returns with a passive index; and table 19 gives the net contribution and market value for company Y's pension assets at the end of each year from 1970 to 1978. A passive index represents a portfolio that seeks to provide investment results corresponding to the price and yield performance of the index under consideration.

In 1970 the fund was heavily invested in equities and real estate. The real estate consisted primarily of a large office building in a major metropolitan area. The remaining 10 percent of the fund was evenly divided between cash and fixed-income securities. In 1970 the common stock was managed externally by four money managers. As table

TABLE 17

ANNUAL RATE OF RETURN ON EQUITY AND FIXED-INCOME PORTFOLIOS OF COMPANY Y, BY MANAGER, 1970–1978

Year	Bank 1		Bank 2		Bank 3, Equity (5)	Adviser 1, Equity (6)	Adviser 2, Equity (7)	Adviser 3, Equity (8)	Index Fund Manager (9)	Internally Managed (10)
	Equity (1)	Fixed income (2)	Equity (3)	Fixed income (4)						
1970	−8.0	—	−6.1	—	—	−4.6	5.0	—	—	—
1971	22.0	—	25.8	—	—	13.0	7.0	—	—	—
1972	21.9	—	28.2	—	—	17.6	8.0	—	—	—
1973	−17.2	—	−22.1	—	—	−19.0	—	—	—	−17.4
1974	−27.7	—	−36.4	—	—	—	—	—	—	−28.0
1975	26.8	—	23.8	9.2	—	—	—	23.0	—	—
1976	12.6	6.4	9.9	10.7	—	—	—	12.2	—	—
1977	−12.6	5.7	—	4.0	−9.3	—	—	−2.0	−7.2	—
1978	9.6	—	—	7.0	4.6	—	—	9.8	6.4	—

SOURCE: Authors.

TABLE 18

COMPARISON OF ANNUAL RATES OF RETURN ON EQUITY AND FIXED-INCOME PORTFOLIOS WITH PASSIVE INDEX, BY MANAGER, 1970–1978

Year	Bank 1 Equity (1)	Bank 1 Fixed income (2)	Bank 2 Equity (3)	Bank 2 Fixed income (4)	Bank 3, Equity (5)	Adviser 1, Equity (6)	Adviser 2, Equity (7)	Adviser 3, Equity (8)	Index Fund Manager (9)	Internally Managed (10)
1970	−12.0	—	−10.1	—	—	−8.6	1.0	—	—	—
1971	7.7	—	11.5	—	—	−1.3	−7.3	—	—	—
1972	2.9	—	9.2	—	—	−1.4	−11.0	—	—	—
1973	−2.5	—	−7.4	—	—	−4.3	—	—	—	−2.7
1974	−1.2	—	−9.9	—	—	—	—	—	—	−1.5
1975	−10.4	—	−13.4	−5.4	—	—	—	−14.2	—	—
1976	−11.2	−12.2	−13.9	−7.9	—	—	—	−11.6	—	—
1977	−5.4	4.0	—	2.3	−2.1	—	—	5.2	0.0	—
1978	3.0	—	—	7.1	−2.0	—	—	3.2	−0.2	—

NOTE: Equity returns are compared with the Standard and Poor's 500 index, and fixed-income returns are compared with Salomon Brothers' long-term corporate bond index. Positive values indicate that the manager earned a return greater than the index, and negative values indicate the reverse.

SOURCE: Authors.

TABLE 19

ANNUAL NET CONTRIBUTION AND MARKET VALUE OF COMPANY Y'S
PENSION ASSETS, 1970-1978

(millions of dollars)

Year	Net Contribution	Market Value
1970	3	92
1971	3	110
1972	7	131
1973	6	116
1974	9	93
1975	7	120
1976	38	172
1977	10	176
1978	32	222

SOURCE: Authors.

17 shows, three of the four equity managers had negative rates of return in 1970. Only one equity manager was able to better Standard and Poor's index in that year (see table 18). In 1970 the real estate component of the fund was appraised at a significantly higher value than it had been. Although the revaluation improved the fund's total rate of return, it is possible that the assigned value could not have been realized by a sale.

Because real estate assets are not continuously traded in an active market, the fund had to use an appraised estimate to determine the real estate's market value. Although appraisals are helpful in estimating market value, they cannot determine the exact sale price of a real asset. Using appraisals as a proxy for market value also makes it difficult to ascertain the total risk of real assets as expressed by their standard deviations. These two problems make the value of real estate within a portfolio difficult to judge.

Table 16 shows that during 1971 and 1972 the equity component of the fund grew in relative value. This increase reflected both the increase in market value of the equities held in 1970 and the additional fund contributions flowing into equities. A strong stock market made continued common stock investment a reasonable choice. As table 18 shows, in both 1971 and 1972 bank managers 1 and 2 had attractive rates of return—greater than the Standard and Poor's index. On the other hand, although the two investment advisers employed by the fund had positive returns, neither was able to outperform the market. On the basis of his inferior performance in 1971 and 1972 in comparison with the other managers, a decision was made to terminate the services of investor adviser 2. The securities that had been managed by him were transferred to the company's treasurer to be managed internally.

In 1973 Standard and Poor's index fell by 14.7 percent. The portfolios of company Y's equity managers fell much further than the index during this year. In the rising stock market of 1971 and 1972, the fund did better than the Standard and Poor's index, and in falling markets the fund did worse. Although such volatile changes indicate that the fund was holding equities more volatile than the market as a whole, this type of equity holding is consistent with the fund's objective of having a portfolio emphasizing growth stocks.

In 1973 the fund's investment strategy stayed largely the same. As we see in table 16, fixed-income securities plus cash constituted about 11 percent of the fund's portfolio. Additional contributions were made primarily to the equity sector of the portfolio, with a slight buildup in cash. The decision was made in 1973 to terminate the services of investment adviser 1 and to consolidate the assets that he had managed with those previously managed internally.

In 1974 the fund was hit hard by the decline in the stock market. As table 19 shows, the market value of the fund's total assets dropped from $116 million to $93 million. The three equity-managed accounts all fell further than the decline of 26.5 percent recorded by the Standard and Poor's index. At the end of 1974, several changes were made: a new equity investment adviser was hired to manage the funds previously handled internally, the company decided to alter the asset allocation mixture of the fund and move additional funds into fixed-income investments, and bank manager 2 was given a portion of the new contributions to invest in the bond market.

In 1975 there was a big comeback in the stock market. Standard and Poor's index was up by 37.2 percent; however, the pension fund in total was up by only 21.2 percent. This wide discrepancy had two causes. First, all three equity managers had returns at least 10 percent below the common stock index return (see table 17). The equity portfolios were no longer performing as high-volatility portfolios might be expected to perform. Instead, the performance reflected a new conservatism by the managers, who had decided to hold less risky stocks. Second, the overall portfolio was, unfortunately, more heavily weighted toward fixed-income investments, which did not perform as well as stocks. At the close of 1975, the market value of the equities held by the fund was down to 57 percent of total portfolio value.

In 1976 there was a further restructuring of the fund's assets. The large real estate asset had to be sold to comply with government regulations. The pension fund might have reinvested in other real estate. Instead, the proceeds were given to bank manager 1 for investment in fixed-income and cash equivalents.

The total return on the fund was 9.6 percent in 1976; return on the Standard and Poor's 500 was 23.8 percent. Again, it was partly the equity accounts of the managers that failed to perform well. In addition, the large portion of the portfolio that was invested in cash equivalents in 1976 contributed to the dismal overall rate of return. Using the treasury bill index as a proxy for the rate of return on cash, the fund's cash assets earned approximately 5.1 percent. In 1976 the investment return performance of both long-term bonds and common stocks exceeded that of treasury bills. In retrospect we can see that the proceeds from the real asset sale were poorly allocated.

In 1977 the stock market declined, and the rate of inflation increased. In an attempt to realize higher returns, the company transferred the equity assets from bank manager 2 to bank manager 3. In addition, $10 million was invested in an equity index fund. The decision to invest in the index fund can be interpreted as an acknowledgment of the need for additional diversification and the desire to earn rates of return on equities that the actively managed fund had not previously earned in comparison to the equity fund index. Bank manager 1 and bank manager 3 did worse than the equity index fund, and investment adviser 3 did better (see table 18). In 1978 the increase in the amount invested in cash equivalents and fixed-income investments (to 48 percent of total assets) helped the pension fund perform better than the common stock index.

In 1978 the fund performed better than the stock market for the third time in nine years. This was primarily the result of the good equity performance by both bank manager 1 and investment adviser 3. In addition, because the treasury bill market outperformed the equity market, the large amount of cash held by the fund contributed to the good record.

During the period 1970–1978, as table 19 shows, there were two unusually large contributions to the pension fund—$38 million in 1976 and $32 million in 1978. The objective of these two large contributions was to prepay a portion of the future expenses of the pension fund and to reduce the unfunded liability. An important implication of this additional funding was the asset allocation decision. It appears that company Y used the contributions to deemphasize the role of equities, preferring to invest in fixed-income and short-term instruments. The memory of the losses in 1974 prevented the fund from maintaining the "aggressive" posture in equities that had originally been one of its stated goals.

Conclusion

The company's pension fund did not achieve its objective of a real rate of return of 3 to 4 percent annually, even though it did achieve its objective of capital preservation and adequate liquidity. The real rate of return actually achieved during the period 1970–1978 was *negative*: −5.2 percent using the CPI index to measure inflation and −4.8 percent with the GNP deflator. The corporation contributed $112 million net from 1971 to 1978, and the total market value rose from $92 million to $222 million, for a capital appreciation of $18 million.

A major reason for company Y's unfortunate investment performance was the poor timing of investment decisions. The timing factor hurt the fund because of the conscious decision to move assets between different types of investment. Table 16 shows that equities ranged from 82 percent to 52 percent of the market value of the pension fund's portfolio. There was no consistently applied asset allocation strategy. The company wanted to maintain flexibility and to have equities ranging from 40 percent to 70 percent of the fund's value. The attempt to time market swings proved incorrect and harmful to the overall value of the fund's assets. When the market declined in 1973 and 1974, the fund moved toward fixed-income investments in 1975 and 1976. If the fund had kept its initial focus on equities throughout the period, the performance would have been much better. The pension fund was following rather than preceding changes in the market and was whipsawed after almost every change that it made.

Another factor that affected investment performance was the inability of the equity managers to match the investment performance of Standard and Poor's index. If the equity component of the pension fund had simply been invested in an equity index fund for the entire period, the annual rate of return on average would have improved by 4 to 5 percent.

The performance of the equity managers demonstrates how difficult it is for the fund to hire managers who outperform the market. Those managers who did outperform the index in one period were not generally able to repeat this performance. The optimal strategy would have been to buy and hold a well-diversified portfolio of equity securities. Higher returns were sacrificed because the pension fund had missed the opportunities afforded by diversification.

The decision not to reinvest the proceeds from the sale of the fund's real estate into real estate also hurt performance. The real estate market began to appreciate at a much faster rate after 1976 than it had before. This decision illustrates two policies pursued by the company during the 1970–1978 period that hindsight, at least, has proved to be incorrect. First, the fund decided in midcourse that real estate was not beneficial. The company's desire for a high degree of liquidity prevented the fund from realizing the potential long-term benefits of including at least some real estate in its portfolio. Second, some real estate (despite its pitfalls), as well as international equities, should probably be included in a well-diversified portfolio. The inclusion of real estate in the portfolio would tend to reduce the risk of the portfolio and might enhance its return, because real estate has shown low correlation with returns on stocks and bonds.

The early policy of minimizing investment in fixed-income securities also proved ill fated. As table 15 shows, the returns on long-term corporate bonds in this period were higher than those on stocks; indeed, real returns on long-term bonds were even slightly positive. The fund sponsor's belief that long-term bonds are unable to keep pace with inflation was unfounded. During this period, it appears, the market had correctly priced long-term bonds, implying that it had made a reasonably accurate guess regarding expected inflation. If a larger proportion of the fund had been held in fixed-income securities, the fund would have been less exposed to the fluctuations in the equity markets. The trend of interest rates was level in this period, however. Long-term bonds may be unable to keep up with inflation if the rate of inflation is rising.

Finally, the fund's managers should have been aware of the difficulties of successfully altering the portfolio mixture. The fund experienced a low rate of return for eight years primarily because of the timing mistakes in asset allocation. In preparing a future strategy, this pension fund, as well as others, should determine the percentage of total assets to be allocated to each type of investment and should then hold to the portfolio mixture selected.

Unfortunately, company Y has not been alone in its mistakes. The results outlined in chapter 4 suggest that this firm had much company. But the aggregated results and this case study point to changes in the allocation of funds among the different types of assets as the primary cause of substandard investment performance.

Notes

1. We thank the corporate treasurer of company Y, who made the data available to us. Since the company wishes to remain anonymous, the data have been disguised. Relations among various pieces of data have not been disguised.

2. These observations are derived from private memorandums prepared by, and circulated among, the finance committee of company Y and from interviews with its chief financial officer.

3. Becker provides securities performance measurements on more than 3,000 equity pension and profit-sharing plans on an annual basis.

4. Indeed, as chapter 6 suggests, there are sensible reasons for placing bonds in a pension portfolio.

5. Roger G. Ibbotson and Rex A. Sinquefield, *Stocks, Bonds, Bills, and Inflation: Historical Returns (1926–1978)* (Charlottesville, Va.: Financial Analysts Research Foundation, 1979).

6
What Can Be Done?

The story told in the last two chapters is a sad one. Pension funds generally performed miserably in relation to inflation: the more actively the managers switched among financial asset categories—the more intensely managers seemed to work to avoid calamitous results—the worse they did.[1] One obvious prescription for pension funds is therefore to adopt an investment strategy in terms of portfolio allocation and to avoid frequent change in that asset allocation. Although this chapter certainly cannot offer any sure-fire approaches to investment strategy for pension funds, it does offer several ideas that may assist pension fund sponsors.

Real Estate

Real estate investment has received increasing attention during the last several years owing to the recent favorable rate of return. In fact, many pension funds are currently dedicating substantial portions of their total portfolios to real estate.[2]

In part such decisions have been stimulated by the recent investment experience in real estate. James R. Webb and C. F. Sirmans, for instance, have documented in great detail the relatively high total returns associated with real estate holdings of various kinds from 1966 to 1977.[3] As table 20 shows, total returns on real estate have been quite impressive when compared with total returns on stock and bond investments. Other research has confirmed these general results using somewhat different measures and data sources.[4]

Several issues must be resolved before we suggest that pension funds should invest in real estate. First, is the real estate market sufficiently deep to warrant investment of large sums by pension funds? The value of pension fund assets approximated $300 billion in 1978; the value of real estate approximated $2.1 trillion in 1978.[5] The market thus seems to be sufficiently large to accommodate the investment of a substantial portion of pension fund assets without disrup-

TABLE 20

RETURNS ON REAL ESTATE AND CAPITAL MARKET INVESTMENTS,
1966–1977
(percent)

Investment	Annual Average Total Return	Standard Deviation
Real estate		
Hotel, motel	12.10	1.17
Elevator apartment	9.59	0.73
Nonelevator apartment	9.63	0.72
Retail (five or fewer stores)	9.53	0.70
Shopping center (more than five stores)	9.58	1.00
Office building	9.58	0.75
Medical office building	9.66	0.74
Commercial warehouse	9.54	0.96
Other commercial	10.36	1.16
Hospital and institutional	11.00	1.33
Industrial warehouse	9.81	0.66
Manufacturing plant	9.70	0.82
Other industrial	9.80	0.86
Capital market		
Common stocks	5.5	19.1
Long-term government bonds	4.1	7.8
Long-term corporate bonds	5.0	9.0
Treasury bills	5.0	1.3

NOTE: The measure of total return employed was as follows:

$$\text{Investment} = \sum_{t=1}^{n} \frac{\text{Before-tax cash flow}_t}{(1+y)^t} + \frac{\text{Before-tax selling price}}{(1+y)^t}$$

where y = rate of return, the rate reflected in the table. Use of the before-tax return is appropriate since pension funds pay no taxes. According to the authors, raw data were obtained from American Council of Life Insurance, "Mortgage Commitments on Multi-family and Non-residential Properties Reported by 15 Life Insurance Companies," No. 774 (May 4, 1978). For returns on capital market instruments, the authors followed the approach of Roger G. Ibbotson and Rex A. Sinquefield, *Stocks, Bonds, Bills, and Inflation: The Past (1926–1976) and the Future (1977–2000)* (Charlottesville, Va.: Financial Analysts Research Foundation, 1977).

For stocks, the return, $R_{m,t} = [(P_{m,t} + D_{m,t})/P_{mt-1}] - 1$, where $P_{m,t}$ is the price at the end of period t, specifically the value of Standard and Poor's 500, and $D_{m,t}$ is the dividend paid on Standard and Poor's 500 stocks during period t. Returns on government bonds and corporate bonds were similarly computed. Data for government bonds and bills were taken from the U.S. government bond file compiled by the University of tion. The second, and by far the more important, question is, How can periodic market values be determined when no active secondary market exists? Periodic valuations are important to the sponsors of pension plans, both to determine how well the pension managers are doing and to assess the cash flow necessary to fund the plan in the future. Finally, there is the question whether real estate investments in the future may reasonably be expected to enjoy the same returns in relation to common stocks and other securities as they have in the past.

Unfortunately this last question cannot be answered with any authority. At the present time, however, real estate may constitute a comparatively poor investment opportunity for tax-exempt pension investors. Real estate investments enjoy some very attractive tax advantages. Purchases of real estate have typically been financed with very high degrees of debt in relation to equity; interest on such debt is a tax-deductible expense for a taxable investor. Although for a pension fund this consideration is not germane, for an individual nudged into increasingly higher tax brackets by the unrelenting thrust of inflation, it serves to encourage the bidding up of property values. Depreciation allowances also offset taxable income, but, again, pension funds cannot exploit this feature. To the extent that inflation stops pushing individual investors into higher tax brackets or corporations into higher effective tax brackets, either because of a reduction in the inflation rate or because of changes in the tax codes, the value of the tax shields associated with real estate investments will stop rising. In light of the most recent changes in the tax code, the effects of which are to cap personal income taxes at 50 percent and to reduce effective corporate tax rates, the potential for capital gains in real estate holdings may diminish in the future. It follows that pension funds may not find succor from the ravages of inflation in real estate investments.

Fixed-Income Investments

Much recent work in financial economics has focused on the effects of personal and corporate taxation on common stocks and bonds in capital market equilibrium, the relative rates of return on stocks and bonds, and the relative costs of capital for corporations from various sources.[6] An outgrowth of that research has shown that pension

---

Chicago's Center for Research in Security Prices. Return data for corporate bonds were derived from the high-grade long-term corporate bond index constructed by Salomon Brothers.
SOURCE: Adapted from Webb and Sirmans, "Yields and Risk Measures," pp. 14–19, tables 4, 5.

funds may be optimally invested solely in taxable fixed-income securities.[7] This prescription is not suggested by considerations of inflation. Given the findings reported in chapter 4, however, investment in short-term fixed-income securities can be assumed to yield returns that tend to keep pace with inflation; so there is a connection.

The shareholders in a corporation may be presumed to hold a mixture of stock and bonds in their portfolios. Given that at least a portion of the return to stock ownership is taxed at capital gains rates, stock returns tend to be more lightly taxed than bond returns, the bulk of which are interest payments taxed at regular rates. Further, shareholders are liable, at least to the extent of their investment, to make up any deficiencies in the pension fund. An aggregate tax saving could be achieved if shareholders held "their bonds" in the pension fund on behalf of corporate employees and reduced individual bond holdings. The net effect would be the placement of the most heavily taxed investment instruments in the most lightly taxed vehicle. Corporate shareholders would, in effect, swap their bond holdings with pension funds for the common stock holdings, and the aggregate tax burden would be reduced.

Irwin Tepper's work is one of the more comprehensive treatments of the issue. Here, in his words, is the argument:

> The return to shareholders [*in the corporation sponsoring the pension plan*] of a debt investment in the pension fund is passed through the corporation and is taxed at the personal tax rate on equities. Hence, so long as the personal tax rate on equities is less than the personal tax rate on debt, shareholders would prefer to have their bond-holdings in the corporate pension fund as opposed to being held in their personal portfolios. . . .
>
> The pension plan should always be funded and debt should be the investment vehicle, so long as personal tax rates on equities are less than that on debt.[8]

A principal reason why Tepper believes that pension funds should be invested in bonds is that bonds are the most heavily taxed investment instrument at the personal level.

Although fully taxable investors should tend to concentrate their portfolio holdings in the least-taxed investments, such as equities and real estate, tax-exempt investors such as pension funds ought to concentrate their holdings in the most heavily taxed instruments, bonds. By following tax arbitrage, pension funds may earn a rent. If such securities earn a rate of return sufficiently high to induce holdings by taxable investors, nontaxed investors can reap an extraordinary return.

The same arguments hold true for individuals who have Keogh plans and individual retirement accounts, both of which have been made more liberal by the Economic Recovery Act of 1981 (which allows larger individual contributions to both). To the extent that these individuals desire to hold both equity and fixed-income instruments in their portfolios, the fixed-income holdings should be concentrated in those accounts that are subject to the least tax.

Fully taxable investors hold shares in many corporations that sponsor pension funds. Is it better for those investors to achieve their own optimal portfolio diversification through the personal holding of bonds or by having the pension funds of those corporations hold bonds? The answer is fairly obvious: taxable investors can reduce their total tax burden by having the heavily taxed bond portion of their portfolios held in the tax-free haven provided by pension funds. Accordingly, fund-held bonds are better than bonds held personally, provided, of course, that bonds would be held in the portfolio anyway.

One prescription for pension funds is therefore "hold bonds." There is no magic to this advice. It merely suggests that the tax collector will take less than otherwise, and this is the source of the benefit that bonds offer sponsors of corporate pension plans and owners of the equity of those corporations.

If the rate of inflation unexpectedly increases and thereby causes the expected rate of inflation to increase, nominal interest rates will rise so as to discount the expected rate of inflation, and the value of all outstanding bonds will decline. Not only will the value of the outstanding bonds held by pension funds decline, but the yields (on par value or cost) from the bonds held by the pension fund will be below current market yields on newly issued bonds. Furthermore, if the rate of inflation becomes high enough, the rate of interest received on the book value of their bond portfolio will be less than the rate of inflation. The sponsoring corporation may, however, hedge against this possibility by funding its pension plan by selling its own debt. As the market value of the pension fund declines, pension fund claims against corporate cash flows increase. At the same time, if the firm has bonds outstanding, their market value also declines. The deficiency in the pension fund can be made up by the sale of additional debt, which substitutes outside claims for pension claims. If such sales are made in the proper amounts, the total real debt claims against the firm can be kept constant; that is, the firm can avoid increased financial risk. In addition, the firm thus enjoys the advantage of a tax deduction on the interest payments on its own debt without paying a tax on the interest income of its pension plan.

If pension plans could protect themselves from unanticipated increases in inflation by holding short-term securities or by creating hedges with long-term bonds, they could be indexed to provide cost-of-living adjustments to retirees already drawing pensions. Feldstein argues, however, that when pension plans eliminate purchasing-power risk to retirees in this way, employees will probably have to be willing to accept lower real pension payments in return.[9] That is, in exchange for less risky pension payments (pension payments indexed against inflation), employees ought to be willing to relinquish some portion of their expected nominal pension payments that would not provide inflation protection.

Suppose now that management of the sponsoring corporation believes stock to provide a more favorable trade-off between risk and expected return than bonds; that is, management may believe common stock to be generally undervalued. In this case, there is still incentive to hold bonds in the pension fund.[10] The sponsor could purchase stock to be held in the corporation and could finance the purchase through the sale of debt. The pension fund pays no taxes on an otherwise heavily taxed financial instrument, but the corporation would still benefit if it discovered and purchased undervalued common stock, the returns on which would be comparatively lightly taxed or not taxed at all if the proceeds from the speculation were placed immediately in the pension fund, hence immediately expensed.

Short-Term Instruments and Commodity Futures

The holding of short-term instruments, for example, treasury bills, will only tend to insulate the value of a pension portfolio from inflation. We say "tend" because sharp, unanticipated changes in inflation will not be immediately reflected in ex ante interest rates. Unanticipated inflation may result in real reductions in the prices of short-term instruments and hence in pension fund values, although the deleterious effect may be comparatively small.

Recent work by Bodie, however, suggests that holding a portfolio reflecting a comparatively large commitment to short-term fixed-income securities and a small commitment to commodity futures contracts can very nearly fully insulate the real value of the pension fund from inflation, provided the returns on the commodity futures contracts are positively correlated with the inflation rates.[11] Indeed, though commodity futures contracts are in themselves quite risky, when they are properly combined with treasury bill holdings, the real risk associated with the portfolio can be lower than for either instrument alone. During the period 1973–1978, for instance, the real annual rates of return on one-month treasury bills, one-year treasury bills, corporate bonds, common stocks, and commodity futures contracts were − 1.62 percent, − 1.57 percent, − 2.83 percent, − 4.19 percent, and 17.72 percent, respectively. Indeed, over the long period 1953–1978 the correlation between the real annual return on commodity futures contracts and inflation was 0.455, suggesting that they serve as quite a good hedge against inflation. In contrast, common stock and twenty-year bond returns experienced correlations of − 0.612 and − 0.404, respectively; they were poor hedges, to be sure.

As everyone knows, commodity futures are quite risky in themselves. When they are combined with other securities holdings, however, commodity futures contracts can reduce the overall risk of the total portfolio. This is because of the negative correlation between returns on commodity futures contracts and those of more traditional financial instruments.[12] Finally, although gains to taxable investors on commodity futures contracts are heavily taxed, pension funds, as we noted above, do not pay any taxes; so this prescription is consistent with the prior one.

International Investment

Many researchers, among them Bruno Solnik, have stressed the significant gains to be achieved by international security diversification.[13] For any given level of risk, higher returns have been achieved through international portfolio diversification than were available from optimally diversified domestic portfolios. Although the prescription was not produced with the goal of protecting real portfolio returns from inflation, it certainly may help.[14]

Pension fund managers in increasing numbers are pursuing international investment opportunities.[15] The pitfalls—potential political instability abroad, perhaps linked to controls that prohibit the repatriation of funds, lack of good financial data on portfolio companies, thin trading markets, and large commission charges—are many, but there is nevertheless a strong prospect that pension funds will perform better with international diversification than without.

Conclusion

This chapter merely makes some suggestions that may be helpful, involving strategies that corporation pension plan sponsors and managers do not now seem to be pursuing. The simplicity of the new investment strategy for pension funds recommended by Tepper and by Black and Dewhurst is striking. Yet in 1981 nonequity investments accounted for only roughly 50 percent of all pension fund assets. The empirical work supporting Bodie's conclusion is preliminary yet most provocative. Nevertheless, pension funds have been notably absent in commodity futures markets, and the reasons are not apparent. Even if pension plan sponsors do not want to pursue the comparatively radical sentiments espoused here, however, the evidence reported in chapters 4 and 5 suggests that they ought not to shift their portfolio allocations among the various investment instruments very often or by great amounts. Those funds that performed best in relation to inflation were those that did not alter portfolio allocations significantly in apparent attempts to time the market.

From the analysis presented in chapter 3, it is not obvious that real returns will be negative on stocks over periods of time longer than those considered in chapters 4 and 5. Our data do show, however, much shifting of the portfolio mixture. It seems that one simple prescription would be for pension fund managers to buy and hold an indexed portfolio, that is, a portfolio that mimics the behavior of the securities markets as a whole. The broadest sort of indexed portfolio would include shares in all traded securities in proportion to the value of each in relation to the aggregate value of the securities markets. More practically, choosing a subset of the stocks constituting Standard and Poor's index would very likely closely approximate the market as a whole. The portion of funds invested in stock would approximately equal the ratio of equity to total capital in the economy, and the remaining funds would be invested in fixed-income instruments. This policy would eliminate active management, which the evidence shows may do more harm than good. To many pension plan sponsors, the notion of an indexed fund may be the most radical suggestion of all.

We have avoided suggesting any changes in pension funding policy or in pension programs or in the way in which pension plans allocate benefits. These matters are important, but they are not the focus of this book. Corporate pension plan sponsors, however, certainly ought to consider changes that might ameliorate the problems caused by inflation; indeed, they must consider all possible options if security markets continue to fail to perform as intuition and theory suggest they should.[16]

We have also skirted two other major issues. First, should pension funds be funded on a pay-as-you-go basis rather than through asset accumulation? Though we have not examined data relevant to this issue, as we stated in chapter 3, we believe that the performance of capital asset markets through the 1970s may have been atypical. Accordingly, we see no clear reason why pension funds should not accumulate designated assets on their own behalf (that is, assets segregated from those of the sponsoring corporation). The rate of return on corporate operating assets—the relevant criterion for a pay-as-you-go system—may not continue to be systematically higher than that on financial (pension) assets. Second, does our evidence suggest in any way that the private pension system concept is inadequate or that private pension funds are no longer viable? Our answer is a resounding no.

Notes

1. Note that pension fund performance was not atypical of managed portfolios. Many investors suffered as much or more during this period.

2. Daniel Hertzberg, "Institutional Investors Turn to Real Estate in Bid to Beat Inflation," *Wall Street Journal*, July 24, 1981.

3. James R. Webb and C. F. Sirmans, "Yields and Risk Measures for Real Estate, 1966–1977," *Journal of Portfolio Management* (Fall 1980), pp. 14–19.

4. Thomas J. Coyne, Waldemar M. Goulet, and Mario J. Picconi, "Residential Real Estate versus Financial Assets," *Journal of Portfolio Management* (Fall 1980), pp. 20–24.

5. Roger G. Ibbotson and Carol L. Fall, "The United States Market Wealth Portfolio," *Journal of Portfolio Management* (Fall 1979), pp. 82–92.

6. For an illustration of this sort of work, see Merton H. Miller, "Debt and Taxes," *Journal of Finance*, vol. 32 (May 1977), pp. 261–75.

7. See Fischer Black, "The Tax Consequences of Long-Run Pension Policy," *Financial Analysts Journal* (July/August, 1980), pp. 21–28; Irwin Tepper, "Taxation and Corporate Pension Policy," *Journal of Finance*, vol. 36 (March 1981), pp. 1–13; and Fischer Black and Moray P. Dewhurst, "A New Investment Strategy for Pension Funds," *Journal of Portfolio Management* (Summer 1981), pp. 26–35.

8. Tepper, "Taxation and Corporate Pension Policy," p. 5.

9. Martin Feldstein, "Private Pensions and Inflation," *American Economic Review*, vol. 71 (May 1981), pp. 424–28.

10. See Black and Dewhurst, "New Investment Strategy for Pension Funds."

11. Zvi Bodie, "An Innovation for Stable Real Retirement Income," *Journal of Portfolio Management* (Fall 1980), pp. 5–13.

12. Zvi Bodie, "Investment Strategy in an Inflationary Environment," Working Paper no. 701 (Cambridge, Mass.: National Bureau of Economic Research, 1981).

13. Bruno Solnik, "Why Not Diversify Internationally, Rather Than Domestically?" *Financial Analysts Journal* (July/August 1974), pp. 48–54.

14. Note that there is some question about the magnitude of the potential gains claimed for international diversification, although there is no doubt that it can be somewhat beneficial. See Dennis E. Logue and Richard J. Rogalski, "Offshore Alphas: Should Diversification Begin at Home?" *Journal of Portfolio Management* (Winter 1979), pp. 5–10, and Dennis E. Logue, "An Experiment in International Diversification," *Journal of Portfolio Management* (Fall 1982), pp. 22–27.

15. Daniel Hertzberg, "Pension Managers Invest More Overseas, Aware of Risks but Hopeful about Profits," *Wall Street Journal,* July 2, 1981, p. 42.

16. Indeed, *Interim Report of the President's Commission on Pension Policy* (Washington, D.C., 1980), favors the inflation indexation of pension benefits. This change, if required by legislation, would necessitate massive changes in the pension system.

Selected AEI Publications

AEI Associates Program

www.ingramcontent.com/pod-product-compliance
Lightning Source LLC
Jackson TN
JSHW011942131224
75386JS00041B/1516